The Miracle of Kindness

Changing the world one act at a time

JAMES R. KOK

Scripture quotations in this publication are from the Holy Bible: New International Version®, NIV®· Copyright© 1973, 1978, 1984 by International Bible Society; the Holy Bible, The Living Bible, Copyright© 1997, 1971 by Tyndale House Publishers, Inc. and the Holy Bible, New King James Version, ® Copyright© 1982, 1980, 1979 by Thomas Nelson, Inc.; The New Revised Standard Version. New York: Oxford University Press, Copyright© 1990. Used by permission.

ISBN 0-615-12747-9
The Miracle Of Kindness
©2005 by James R. Kok.

Published by James R. Kok
12141 Lewis St.
Garden Grove, California 92840

Cover design by Craig Bourne
Discussion Guide by Craig Bourne

For more information or to order additional copies,
please contact James R. Kok
(714) 971-4031
jimkok@crystalcathedral.org

Other Books by James R. Kok

90% Of Helping Is Just Showing Up!

Waiting For Morning

Family At Work

The Pastoral Counselor Treatment Planner

No Such Thing As Over The Hill

Dedicated to-

Jonah

Meghan

Silas

Larkin

Simon

Alice

Six—whose vitality, beauty and energy motivate me
to greater expressions of Care and Kindness.

CONTENTS

Acknowledgments

The Becomers Class (past President Ken Waltz and Anne, current President Larry La Bonte and Judy) is the adult fellowship group where Linda and I find support, encouragement, and pleasant friendship. They have supported this book every way needed and made its publication possible.

Craig T. Bourne, Editor, and composer of the Discussion Guide, has worked tirelessly, volunteering world-class skill to shape this book. Craig has seen to it that this book was born.

The "Care and Kindness Conference" leaders—Debbie Bourne, Pete and Jan Petereit, David Thompson, Art Gebhart, Nancy Vander Plas, Loretta Conrad, Dan Whedon, Dorothy McCrory, Donna Grimm, Shirley Zink, and Susan Balk have been strong companions in this entire venture.

Bev Michielson believes more than anybody in the value and good of this campaign. She is our inimitable advocate everywhere she sings and speaks.

Glenn De Master is always an enthusiastic encourager.

Linda Kok has been a consistent consultant and perspicacious critic.

Kathryn Schaap Kok, my mother, showed me a life of hospitality, kindness and love in the brief fifteen years of my life with her.

The people of the Crystal Cathedral Congregation who so conspicuously and consistently show loving-kindness.

Introduction

I was destined to write this book on Care and Kindness.

My mother died long before I began asking questions about my young life. Mothers remember little things, but I missed that opportunity. My Dad, however, did recall one tidbit that confirms the destiny idea—he said that whenever I woke up, already as a wee infant, even in the middle of the night, I would give a big smile.

Those who know me are aware of a streak of cantankerousness in me, too, but mostly I think I have been compelled toward kindness and consideration. I like people and I want to treat them in a way that encourages and communicates that they are valued. I like to connect with people, hear their stories, lift their spirits. I want to be appreciated and thought well of. All of this is the way God has prepared and qualified me for this campaign to increase Care and Kindness.

I believe the nature that God implanted in me is intended to equip, inspire and motivate followers of Jesus to let the goodness in their hearts express itself. My calling is to convince others they are qualified and needed to act in this world to make God look good.

This sense of God-guided destiny includes my challenging and rewarding twenty years at the Crystal Cathedral. There is no place on earth more suited for living out a passion to equip and motivate followers of Jesus for greater output of Care and Kindness.

More than anything else, the Schullers, who founded this world-wide ministry, want to brighten lives, encourage the uncertain and inspire the struggling and straggling.

The Care and Kindness campaign is a reflection of what the Crystal Cathedral ministry is about. We are endeavoring on the individual basis to equip and motivate God's people to become self-aware, intentional, hope-building ambassadors of encouragement and confidence-building.

Last Chance!

The traditional church has one last opportunity to win the world. Winning is possible if every individual follower of Jesus sees it as his personal responsibility to boldly let the love of Jesus within spill out everywhere he goes.

Christianity is not appealing to the rank and file unchurched American: they do not like Christians. We must change that! And we can, if every pulpit and Bible Study, Small Group and writer includes the mandate we stress again and again in this book: *"You are the light of the world...let your light shine before men, that they may see your good deeds and praise your Father in heaven."* The bottom line of each message of every Christian gathering must be to motivate each other toward sparkling living: encouraging, appreciating, cheering, listening, and so much more—all of which we speak in this book.

Talking is almost over for Christians. We have not lived up to our words. Actions, exemplary behavior, and Care and Kindness are desperately needed. Every man, woman and child is a qualified deliverer of Jesus' love. Even if you are 103 years old or a Down Syndrome person, you can give a smile or a hug. Everybody is able.

This book is intended to help make it happen. It is designed to inspire you and motivate you in **The Miracle of Kindness**; to help unleash the Spirit of Jesus so "They will know we are Christians by our love."

Jim Kok
December 2004

-1-

They Will Know We Are Christians By Our Love

There is so much more that followers of Jesus can do. Every day is packed with opportunities. Every person we meet needs a word, a touch, a smile—a lift. Care and Kindness is the love of God, the Spirit of Jesus, flowing through us. There are friends to call, neighbors to visit, sick to write to, and injured to pray for.

The Miracle of Kindness is more than a book. It is a zealous prayer to ignite people with a passion to brighten the world. It is so needed. It is so good. It is so possible.

Miracles of Kindness: they are happening all around you. If you look for them, you will see them— to your left or right, or even right in front of you.

Opening the cracker wrapping

Jan Judd Petereit was visiting her Centenarian Mother at the nursing home. They were having lunch together when Jan noticed at an adjacent table another elderly resident fumbling futilely with a cellophane soda cracker package. So Jan got up from her chair, went over and opened it for the lady.

Says Jan, *"For the rest of my visit, the lady kept waving at me with a big smile on her face, like I'd given her a major prize."*

Sometimes miracles of kindness are the result of a conscious act by a sensitive person. Kathleen from Mesa, AZ reports this story:

Merely reaching out

While sitting in the doctor's waiting room, I noticed a woman across from me was crying. When the chair beside her became empty, I sat beside her, gave her some tissues, and said, *"Seeing your tears makes my heart ache for you. I don't know what the trouble is, but I want you to know I care."*

Through her tears, this woman told me she was in a great deal of pain from an ear infection. I told her how sorry I was that she felt so badly, that it was a good thing she had come to the doctor, and that I hoped she would soon feel better.

And there are times when the intention is good, but mistakes are still made. This little story has a humorous twist.

Oops

The moving truck loaded with furniture was parked in front of our Southern California home. My husband and I were sweeping out our garage, with the door open, when a woman from across the street approached with an apple pie.

"Welcome to the neighborhood," she said with a smile. *"I baked it myself and I want you to have it."*

"Really, we can't," my husband replied.

"Of course you can," she ran on. *"When I moved in two years ago, no one welcomed me, and I want you to feel at home."* She thrust the pie into my husband's hands.

"Uh, well, you see," he stumbled, with an embarrassed laugh, *"we've been here four years and we're moving out."* The woman stared at him, dumbfounded, her mouth open. *"Well,"* she said, shrugging her shoulders with an air of resignation, *"enjoy it anyway!"*

My husband and I laughed heartily, enjoyed the pie, and resolved in the future to be better neighbors.

The point of our Christian faith is to turn us into grateful ambassadors of God's goodness. In the first anecdote above, we see Jan being attentive to the plight of someone nearby. Some might not have noticed the elderly woman's struggling—considered it as "normal". But one of the core conditions of being a caring person is observing and paying attention to others. Then, taking action where a need is obvious, as Jan did.

The transformation into ambassadors of goodness involves a determined conviction that God is alive and loving His creation. Those revolutionized by this spiritual reality are then inspired to do everything they can to improve this life for those around them—both present and future. In the second anecdote, we see the caring person, Kathleen, willing to reach out to another who is hurting. She noticed. She moved over. She gave tissues. She said a few words. So simple. So possible. So needed. So lovely!

This kindness is what followers of Jesus Christ are expected to strive toward, to incorporate into their everyday lives, and to deliver.

There are endless possibilities. Every last follower of Jesus can participate in and help with simple down-to-earth acts of Care and Kindness.

There is a lot more, of course!

The bigger gifts

There is the gigantic part of doing one's daily work with carefulness, honesty and integrity.

There is the wonderful need for people to beautify and entertain and inspire through music, and all the arts.

There is the overwhelming challenge of saving and improving lives through medical care and scientific discovery. Every industry, from transportation to astronomy, from education to construction, is equally called to glorify God by making this world a better place.

There is also something that comes before, after, and during all the vocational challenges we have. This "something" is a direct and immediate way of letting God out of your heart and into someone else's life through Care and Kindness. It is possible! It is possible for every man, woman and child, every hour that we are awake.

God is love and every act of Care and Kindness we exhibit is a kind of giving birth to God in that moment. Loving kindness is giving tastes of God to the unsuspecting, to anonymous strangers, to anyone in our sphere of influence or just along our path, and to friends and family. Even when it is not named as coming from The Source Of All Love, loving kindness is nevertheless a gift of God that helps all who receive it or are touched by such a gift in some form.

We are called to suffer

Being a follower of Jesus is not just about having a ticket to heaven. It is not just about feeling forgiven, saved, redeemed or thankful. It is not simply about feeling anything, even though powerful feelings may nourish one's spiritual life.

It is about knowing you are a precious child of God who is needed and who has gifts that The Lord needs you to use. Being a follower of Jesus is to be willing to work hard— even suffer to help God get His message and his Goodness into the world.

St Paul said this:

> ...those who are led by the Spirit of God
> are children of God...
> and if children, then heirs,
> heirs of God and joint heirs with Christ—
> if in fact we suffer with him...
> **Romans 8:14–16**

Paul says, "Suffer with him." To suffer with Christ means—at the very least—to be going about our everyday business intentionally taking risks to deliver concrete acts and words of Care and Kindness. According to those words of St. Paul, inclusion in the family of Jesus Christ involves a lifestyle that thinks of others and thoughtfully sacrifices one's personal comfortableness in strategic ways at strategic times to deliver goodness, love, support, and encouragement to others. This is a form of suffering to which we are called.

We may need our minds blown open for this. It is a revolutionary change for many to decide to do what is uncomfortable.

It means that a trip to the bank is not just to deposit money.

It is to notice people and find ways to lift their spirits.

A trip to the Post Office is not just to buy postage stamps.

It is a trip to stand in line and sensitively endeavor to connect with the person next to you and find a way to bless him or her through a word, a listening ear, or a smile.

When back-fence chatter informs you that the couple across the street is going through a divorce or loss of job, the follower of Jesus hears a mandate to send a message or to show up with a spirit-lifting visit—even when you have no idea how to help, what to say, or perhaps even who they are. That is part of the suffering with Christ to which we are called.

Loving kindness can be very hard

Here's a story that illustrates this. It is an example of rare courage, as Marilyn Duff takes a deep breath and moves into an extremely foreboding situation because she knows it is the right thing to do.

I hardly ever went to funerals or wakes. My childhood had been full of deaths in our family, including two brothers, whose deaths had filled our home with grief for years. I had a terrible aversion to others' displays of grief, remembering my parents' pain. I'd learned that I couldn't hold back my own tears when confronted by another's grief, and I hated to cry in public.

Then, one afternoon, I read in the papers about a young man in Texas who had shot his new wife and then killed himself. I was shocked to recognize the name as a neighbor's son, a boy I'd watch grow up, play ball in the street, wait tables in a nearby restaurant. David was always polite, never embarrassed to respond to a wave, a smile, or a hello from an adult.

His mother was one of those neighbors whom you stop and chat with in the produce department of the supermarket, have a brief conversation when you meet in the ice cream parlor, or laugh together over some neighborhood incident. Not a close friend, but close enough that I was appalled at this terrible news, and I knew I should go and see her.

I tried to fight off that impulse. I don't know her well enough, I rationalized. She wouldn't want to see anyone but family. It might look like morbid curiosity if I went down there.

But a voice in my head said, "You know what a mother's grief is like. You watched your own mother when a son died. You must go."

It was twilight when I donned a sweater and walked down the darkening street. Panic filled me. What would I say? How would the parents be? Would they have a relative answer the door to tell me to go away? "Please, God, help me to find the words," I found myself praying.

On the porch I rang the bell. The older brother opened the door. I did not know him at all. I identified myself and asked if I could come in. His mother was sitting on the couch. At the sound of my voice, she got to her feet and hurried toward me. "Marilyn," she said, "how nice of you to come."

And without thinking I stepped inside, opened my arms and took her in. We held each other like that for a few minutes, and I realized that we were both shaking with stifled sobs. Tears ran down my cheeks. I am hopeless, I thought. Hopeless at this. "I'm so sorry," I said, "so very sorry."

Then she led me to a couch as I fished for a tissue. "Here," she said. "Sit down."

She watched me as I dabbed at my eyes. She was doing the same. I said, "Your son was a special boy, Linda. I've known a lot of teenagers, and he stood out because he was always so friendly."

"Oh! You knew him?"

"Well...yes, I did." I had no idea what I was going to say next but I knew I had to say something. She was peering at me intently. "When my husband and I drove down the street and he and his friends were playing ball in the middle of it, he always moved over, and waited respectfully. He would wave if I waved at him, you know, a neighborly kid. Just a kid, but nice."

"Oh." She smiled, through her tears. "Yes."

"And when he was in high school and worked at the Sizzler, he used to wait on our table sometimes. He always let us know that he knew

we were neighbors, and he smiled and passed the time of day before he took our order. He was so mature for his age, and so..." I grasped for words, hardly knowing what I was saying, "sweet. He was just a very sweet boy."

Her face, wet with tears, shone as though I had given her a great gift. She grasped my hand. "Thank you for telling me that, Marilyn. I had no idea you knew him! No idea!"

I was stunned at the depth of her gratitude, and relieved beyond measure. I realized then that what I had given her was a view of her son that no one else had. And it was a gift to her. The only gift I had to give her. If I had kept it to myself, it would have done no one any good. But to her, it was another memory she could keep the rest of her life of how her boy had touched others' lives. We talked more, and I let her do most of it. She wanted to go over the terrible tragedy, but not in great detail. After a decent interval, I found a place where I could excuse myself. As she walked me to the door, I asked if there was anything I could do for her, immediately, or in the weeks to come. No, she said, it was just so nice that I had come. I told her to call me if she needed to talk; she said she would and I left.

When I made my way alone up the dark street, I felt so light. Even with my eyes still damp from tears I had feared to shed, I knew I had done the right thing. And I thanked God for being there to help me find the words. **Marilyn Duff**

Our mission

I am convinced that Christian people can be inspired and motivated to higher levels of kind and loving behavior in everyday life. So that <u>They will know we are Christians by our love</u>, I am motivated to spread the vision of Care and Kindness. My God-given mission is to fan the flames of love in the hearts of Jesus followers and hopefully start a prairie fire of conspicuous deeds, actions and behaviors that will make the world a better place. I want to inspire and convince good people to do a little more, consistently, and intentionally. I want them to go into difficult places where the hurting, the sick, the bereaved are. More than that, I want them to be sprinkling kindness everywhere they go—on everyone, including those who do not necessarily look needy and discouraged.

Here's another story that touches on the urgency of the need to equip and inspire followers of Jesus to new and better levels of thoughtful Care and Kindness.

> Debbie Bourne was sitting in the airport lounge, overhearing the pleasant chatting of the women sitting nearby and she soon established that they were all Christians. Debbie ventured a few contributions and questions into their discussion, but she was also engrossed in the Harry Potter novel she had brought along. At one point one of her new friends asked, *"What are you reading?"* And Deb answered, *"Harry Potter."*
>
> At that answer, the air chilled noticeably, Deb says. The nearby woman obviously disapproved of her reading material and sent the message by pulling back from her.

The cool silence was finally broken when the woman asked further, *"Have you read the **Left Behind** series of books?"*

"No," answered Deb, *"but my husband and daughter have."* That answer seemed to reassure the questioner and a bit of warmth returned to her countenance.

This incident is an example of how the church needs to change. Overall, the Christian church is an incredibly positive gift to the world. Its influence has made the world a better place by far—more than it would otherwise have been. But individual Christians continue to give Christianity a reputation as a judgmental, self-righteous, holier-than-thou organization. Those who create this unattractive scenario are a small minority. Most are kind, considerate and thoughtful. The few, like the Harry Potter hater, spread the negative picture millions focus on and use to firm up their opinions of Christians in general. It should be possible to hold a different value and still exhibit warmth toward those who see life differently.

So, to help us move towards the goal of being easily recognized as followers of Jesus—so that the world will indeed know us by our love—the following chapters have been created to provide you with details, illustrations, and examples of how you can be part of this movement. You will find tools and guidelines to better equip you as you reach out to be a care GIVER to people all around. You will discover the guiding principals and theological truths on which this mission of Care and Kindness is built and by which it is fueled and strengthened.

Heartwarming examples

But before we move on, let's look at several illustrations. Here are some positive actions certain people have taken:

1) I learned recently of a group of six women who make a point of attending funerals and memorial services at mortuaries and churches. They watch for notices in the newspaper and elsewhere, then they find the locations. They show up at certain ones: those that they have been told will be attended by only a handful of family members.

The reason they participate like this is the result of having noticed that these important events are such weak experiences when only a few are there to take part. When only the immediate family is sitting down front to say farewell to their beloved dad or mom, death seems to have the last word. So the six strangers make a point to lustily join in on the prescribed litanies, responsive readings, communal prayers and hymns. They want to create a strong sound to the Lord, to speak out on behalf of the bereaved, to make a joyful noise of hope and future life. <u>Six caring women, fueled by the love of Christ, giving unique gifts to friends they have never met.</u>

2) While reading a popular book, **The Secret Life of Bees**, by Sue Monk Kidd, I was touched by a simple sentence about one of the characters, June, who plays the cello. She "played music for dying people, going to their homes and even to

the hospital to serenade them into the next life."
Another creative venture full of loving kindness.

3) It reminds me of a man nearing retirement who is starting a practice of supplying recorded music and a boom box to Hospice patients coming to the end of their earthly lives. He says the idea came to him from contemplating what he would like when that time arrives in his life. He realized he'd like to be surrounded night and day by Handel's music. So he reasoned others would like something similar and a ministry of loving kindness was born.

4) Bonnie Bowman was early to a committee meeting, so she sat in her car reading for a little while. A car pulled in next to her and when Betty turned to look; her eyes met the eyes of another woman. Betty smiled and turned back to her book. Two minutes later there was a tap on her window. Betty opened it and the woman, slightly tearful, thanked Betty for her smile. She then related some of the difficulties of that day and said how much the smile had healed her discouragement and lifted her heart. Kindness can be so simple.

5) The famous actress, Marilyn Monroe, was once asked if she felt love from any of the many foster families with whom she lived. She replied, *"Once, when I was 7 or 8. The woman I was living with was putting on makeup and I was watching her. She was in a happy mood, so she reached over and patted my cheeks with her rouge* *puff. For that moment, I felt loved by her.* "A very simple action, like patting a little girl's cheek, can send a message of love.

Heart-tugging stories like these are countless, but there's a sadness in them, too. Good people are making a difference all the time, everywhere. God is working through his people round the clock. The world is much better because the Spirit of Jesus is flowing in the lives of human beings. Some know Him, and some do not know where their thoughtfulness originates. They display goodness in their lives but fail to realize that it comes from another source, the God of Love. Thank God that He has planted the seeds of love in every human heart. Followers of Jesus are called to consciously brighten this world. They know and love the source of the light.

When love failed to show

But, sad to say, the opposite kinds of behaviors also are going on. Good people are not above their flaws and inconsiderateness. Let's look at a few examples from the flawed side:

1) First, one of the most jarring laments I've heard:

> It came from a young mother whose first child was born with Down Syndrome—a difficult assignment for the parents, right from the start. But the heartache twisted tightly the first Sunday morning they brought the little one to the church nursery and carefully placed her in one of the cribs. There were a half dozen other mothers present, ooohing and aahing over each other's perfect babies. But not one crossed the room to adore her newborn. They stayed away. And it hurt. Their avoidance of her and her beloved

baby sent a painful message of rejection that she felt sharply for herself and the baby.

<u>She had hoped it would be different with followers of Jesus.</u>

2) Another story was shared with me by one of my colleagues in ministry:

> He told me about friends he and his wife enjoyed who were single mothers. Several of them earned a living as waitresses in a restaurant near a large church. They were unanimous with their opinion that they disliked working on Sunday, at noon. The reason caught me off balance. On Sunday noon, they said, most of their patrons are those who have been in church the hour before and now come for a meal. These folks, they agreed, were the most demanding, rude, unkind, and stingiest tippers of all their customers, all week long.
>
> <u>Their impression of God's people was mostly negative, of course.</u>

3) This one is not an example of failure in kindness but instead is a summation by a man who apparently had experienced and observed disappointing behavior on the part of Christians.

> A half-dozen years ago, this man I knew slightly, announced he was disillusioned with Christians. They are no better than anyone else, he explained. In spite of decades of sermons, Bible study and fellowship with each other, those who never come near houses of worship behave just as well, if not better, he declared. I did not dispute his claim,

even though I found it enormously troubling and arguable. He didn't need an argument.

He needed some evidence he was mistaken.

This book is part of my life's mission to prove that skeptic wrong by awakening, recruiting, motivating and urging God's people to do better. Here is a subtle illustration of how, by just being kind and interested, people can make a life-changing difference in another's life.

This is Don Heinlein's account of how he was changed at the Crystal Cathedral:

Good Folks Change Two Lives

I guess if I were standing before Christ and pleading my case I would probably say the following:

The first 51 years of my life was a wasteland of unhappiness, bitterness, and negative existence. Depression tormented me to where suicide sometimes seemed a real option. I never felt any real love for or from anyone and, no doubt, I must have been a pretty scary guy to my wife and two children. I never cared much for my mother or father for most of those 51 years. The late singer Peggy Lee's song, "Is That All There Is?" often echoed through my mind and I related to it. The friends we had were not very genuine either.

My Mom was a good person, as others saw her. I once overheard her tell others how my birth had caused her so much pain in the delivery room. An Aunt who died while I was still an infant would hold me and look down at me and say "He's going to be a real heartbreaker." (This was told to me many times by my Mother, and I apparently accepted that as a negative prophecy!)

When I was 5 or 6 years old, my parents bought a small 63-acre farm east of Cincinnati. My brother and I were left at home while Mom worked at a defense plant and my Dad worked as a carpenter. One Sunday, the family visited a small church nearby and after a few visits, I found myself in a summer Vacation Bible School. I'll never forget how caringly and lovingly I was treated by those wonderful ladies at the church. One day, my Dad learned that the front door of the church needed work, so Dad volunteered to repair it. Since he worked 6 days a week, he repaired it on a Sunday afternoon. A few days or weeks later, he was publicly criticized by some Elder or Deacon for working on Sunday. Our family left the church with the attitude, "If that's how the so-called Christians act, then forget it!" The result was no further enthusiasm for church.

Mom was really into controlling and was quick to start slapping, beating and using sarcasm as a quick fix to correcting behavior problems. She, too, was on the negative slope of life. I never quite understood her anger until after she died. Mom's one and only sister, who also was the brunt of her cruelty, finally told me about their Father. The five children were raised in the hills of Kentucky. She said the Father's anger lashed out on the kids with beatings from the same straps that were used on the horses. He even hurled fist-sized rocks at the boys. My Mom managed to leave home at an early age and found my Dad. My Aunt said Mom was never permitted to go to town with her brothers, since she was needed on the farm. So she decided that if she got a chance to get away from home, she would marry the first man she met, just to get away from home, and she did.

At this point, I began to understand a lot about my own collateral damage. To help myself, I spent hours and hours reading books and listening to audiotapes on psychology and self-improvement, with a small margin of success.

The Miracle of Kindness

There was a change in my life in 1989, when my wife and I began attending the Crystal Cathedral. After just a few visits, I could clearly see a change in her, as well as in myself. I even found it gratifying that some of our half-ass friends dumped us because we found Christ. When we attended the Crystal Cathedral, people were so kind to us and never judgmental. We also discovered that they, too, wrestled with many similar things in their lives. I noticed that my anger and other bad habits began to diminish. Our marriage changed to a point where we really, really loved each other more than we had ever before.

One day, Warren Nelson walked up to us and began talking to us. He invited us to the Homebuilders adult fellowship class. We accepted his offer and we found even more great people there. It was the door that I had been searching for all my life. What a blessing!

Nothing dramatic was ever said to us in the whole process of our change. It was a matter of just being around kind, thoughtful, interested, humorous and friendly followers of Jesus, who were our age. Both of us became more sensitive ourselves, in ways we had missed before. Pat began caring for children in our home, whereas previously, both of us had felt we were lacking in skill and confidence around children.

In March 97, my wife Pat suddenly died in her sleep. Thank God, good people at the Crystal Cathedral were there for me. **Don Heinlein**

Don Heinlein today is a Teddy Bear who generously helps anyone who asks with a computer problem. He reaches out to other men and takes them on sailing trips, meets for breakfast with a small group of peers and enjoys a new marriage.

His story is so powerful for all of us. To realize that our routine conversations, asking about another's family or work, playful jousting and jesting, friendship and compassion, in the context of Christian living, makes a difference. It can be life changing, as it was for Don and Pat.

Let's increase the light

When we combine the loving creative ideas that inspire us with the negatives that embarrass and sadden us, we have a strong call for action. Followers of Jesus are obligated to do better. We need to be conspicuous and renowned for sharing hope, care, appreciation, and encouragement, personally, day after day. Jesus said, "You are the light of the world." This is a powerful statement. It means the goodness in the human race, like hopefulness and enthusiasm to build and improve our world, is dependent on the inspiration, healing, compassion and creativity of

God's people. The light others enjoy is brightened by the lives of Jesus' people diligently caring for all of creation.

Small starts, big results

Someone has claimed that the infinitesimal air turbulence caused by a butterfly can initiate bigger breezes, then winds, followed by weather changes, leading to storms and finally hurricanes. An incredible thought, but when it comes to simple acts of Care and Kindness, it is true. Small acts by little known people can set off a chain reaction of goodness that is world changing. The most phenomenal changes on earth have flowed from the life, love, death and resurrection of Jesus. We, his followers, are called to build on his enormous goodness, to keep His love alive. That is what it means to be "the light of the world."

To switch metaphors, we want to cause a ripple that will grow into a mighty wave of Care and Kindness, washing across our continent so boldly that "they will know we are Christians by our love."

I am strongly encouraged in this mission by the founding Pastor of The Crystal Cathedral, who constantly says in his prophetic messages words like this:

"All my life I have worked for
and dreamed that followers of Jesus would
be seen as the nicest of all people."
Robert H. Schuller,
Sunday sermon January 30, 2001

Religion that God our Father accepts
as pure and faultless is this:
to look after orphans and widows in their distress
and to keep oneself from being polluted by the world.
James 1:27

Discussion questions for Chapter 1 are on pages 223–225.

꤮꤮꤮꤮꤮꤮꤮

Kindness Example

Meghan T. Anderson, age 9, loved her beautiful blond curls and cherished the way they hung down her back in gentle ringlets. But then she heard of a need by children who have lost their own hair through chemotherapy treatments. With joy, and slight distress, she pledged to let hers grow until it was ten inches long. Then she would have it cut and mailed to "Locks of Love". "Locks of Love" is a non-profit cause that collects hair to be made into wigs and extensions for these children with cancer.

Reflection: The "slight distress" Meggie felt as she went ahead with her commitment makes her gift even better. By parting with her hair painfully, the deed becomes more truly sacrificial. This kind of giving is a minor, but estimable, form of dying for another person.

꤮꤮꤮꤮꤮꤮꤮

ഗ~ഗ~ഗ~ഗ~ഗ~ഗ~ഗ

Kindness Example

Anette took her beloved pet dog to the groomer for its summer haircut and trim. She rested in the customer waiting area for the job to be completed.

She was so thrilled with the results that she spent a couple of minutes writing a note of appreciation to the groomer. She left the note at the cash register as she checked out and paid her bill.

A short time after arriving home, the phone rang. It was the groomer. She was in tears with gratitude for Anette's note. *"No one has ever done that before,"* she said. She was overwhelmed with her feelings of thankfulness for Anette's thoughtfulness."

Reflection: This is so amazing. When you do something like Anette did, you assume it to be a common gesture offered frequently. So it is stunning to learn that compliments and appreciation are so rarely offered.

ഗ~ഗ~ഗ~ഗ~ഗ~ഗ~ഗ

Kindness Example

Jonah, Meghan, Silas and I attended a stirring presentation of the musical **Godspell** and were exiting the theatre after a standing ovation for the cast. At the rear of the Montague playhouse, off to the side, I noticed two men, dressed mostly in black uniforms, standing by the spotlights used in the performance. Apparently, they had managed the lighting all evening. Now they were chatting with each other, unnoticed by the departing crowd.

Realizing the important but inconspicuous role the two men had played, I leaned toward them and said, *"Great job with the lights tonight."* That lit them up. They beamed with appreciation. It was obvious that they rarely received acclaim for their behind-the-scenes task.

Reflection: How many craftsmen and helpers are behind-the-scenes? That is where most are—inconspicuous and overlooked! A little extra effort can find them and affirm them.

-2-

Five Key Essentials to Encourage and Motivate

A strong motivating conviction generated these **Five Keys**. For forty years, I have been working in the "pool of pain": with and around God's people who have been hurt, devastated, diagnosed, and afflicted by adverse and horrific circumstances, illnesses, losses, rejections and failures.

In most cases, I have been present to them as a Pastor, endeavoring to contribute something that might directly or indirectly support them. In most cases, I tried to "walk with them" as they reeled and staggered, groped, fell down and got up again. It is not hard for me to admit to a profound feeling of helplessness and empty-handedness almost all the time, in nearly every instance.

One stunning discovery has come out of all this. In almost every case, sooner or later, God has lifted them back to their feet, propped them up, and got them going again. I attribute this remarkable fact to God's healing presence. This Divine Care and Kindness can be anticipated and relied on by those hit by freight trains and bulldozers—God does restore even the most smashed.

God needs our help

This is so important that it not only gives a strong encouragement to all who surround the crushed, but it mandates something else: each of us in our heartfelt and heartbroken empathy and sympathy need not be overwhelmed by the thought that we have to find ways to make other folks better again. We must "walk with them" — but with a tremendous sigh of release, we can trust God to put them back together. God needs our help, but God will take care of the healing, in God's time and in God's way.

The strong motivating conviction behind the **Five Keys** is that <u>people are needed!</u> They do not need to be skilled helpers or highly qualified caregivers. But they do need to "show up". They do need to "walk along with" the injured and bereaved. And every last human being qualifies as a healer/helper in the challenge of helping God in the restoration and re-building process. The **Five Keys** must be incorporated into the hearts of all followers of Jesus because they will provide confidence and assurance for the task and challenges that are all around us all the time.

The **Five Keys** are not just for helping the terribly hurt. They are for everyday use with cashiers, colleagues, carwash men and delivery truck people. As you read them, you will visualize endless opportunities for bringing God to people through simple acts of Care and Kindness, every day of the week. Here is an example of how that can be accomplished:

> When shopping at a gigantic craft and art show, Barry made a point of stopping at as many of the two hundred booths as he could. At each booth he thanked the owner, who was usually the artist who had created the objects for sale. He said, *"Thank*

you for making the world a more beautiful and interesting place by crafting your art so nicely." The artists were usually caught off guard at first, but after it registered in their consciousness, they glowed with appreciation for the kind words.

Barry did this because he had changed his mental spectacles earlier. Instead of seeing merchants wanting to take his money, he saw artists making their work available. Now he realized they were creative persons deserving appreciation and needing encouragement. Barry commended them when he reflected how folks like these enriched his habitat, for every piece that they designed and produced was wrapped with their passion, and their self-esteem clung to each as well. He found his praise and support was taken in like nourishment and water to hungering and thirsting souls.

What a lot of pleasure Barry delivered that day. If he had purchased something at every artist's booth, he wouldn't have done as much good as he did. These people deserved every word of his praise and rarely got a lot from the browsing patrons. What he did could be done by anyone.

Read now the **Five Keys** and thoughtfully apply them to yourself.

Essential Key #1: I have the capacities, qualities and abilities that can brighten another's life, or help them face challenges.

There is no one so young or so old, so poor, homely, mentally deficient or uneducated that they can't encourage another. Every living human being can lift another's spirits somehow. No one is disqualified.

In my first year of ordained ministry, I served in a large psychiatric state hospital in Gowanda, New

York. My duties included bringing a message every Sunday morning to a large crowd of patients. The routine had me standing at a main door greeting the exiting people after the service concluded. As the people left on my first morning preaching, one man grabbed my hand with both of his and said something I could not understand. But his nodding and his smile seemed to indicate appreciation. It was a brief and relatively meaningless encounter. On the following Sunday, the same thing happened. And my very brief pause to acknowledge him was the same as before. Dozens were passing by, either saying something or not. I gave them each a quick touch and a smile.

On my third Sunday, "the man" came by again. Same routine, but I thought I detected his sounds as saying, *"Good sermon, Pastor."* My response was, as before, very brief, but by the fourth Sunday, I was looking forward to "the man" and his body language that approved of my work. I realized he had been blessing me. Now I was looking forward to it, needing it.

I learned he was brain damaged and psychotic, controlled with a lot of medication. Nevertheless, it didn't matter to me what was broken in his system, I appreciated his weekly gift to me and I looked forward to it every week for the whole year I was there. His appreciation and my neediness taught me an important lesson: Anyone can encourage another. Everyone has the capacity to lift the spirits of someone else.

Every child of God, and that includes every little boy or girl as well as adults, has within him a whole lot of love that those around us need. When Jesus said, "The Kingdom of God is within you," he was referring to those qualities from the Holy Spirit we carry with us and are obliged to shed wherever we go. Each of us, no matter how young or old, has good things to give to others that they need. This is the first step in helping the Kingdom to come on earth as it is in heaven. Loving, caring kindness is creating a more heavenly atmosphere in this human world we are part of, and we all can add to it. Here we see the Miracle of Kindness at work.

Essential Key #2: Everyone needs my encouragement and support. People need to be noticed personally and respectfully by me and given some word, gesture, or look of appreciation.

The second important learning I gained from "the man" at the door who offered understandable but unintelligible blessings was how much I needed affirmation and encouragement. It is not an extreme stretch to generalize from my own hungers to realize that other people are just like me.

For fifteen years as a chaplain at Pine Rest Mental Health Services, I usually left my door open for the first hour of the day. Part of this was motivated by a pattern that had developed. A young woman named Glenda, with Down Syndrome, came by daily on a work assignment. She always stopped, looked in, waved and smiled with a warm greeting. I came to depend on her daily blessing and my warm response, no doubt, insured her daily stop because it strengthened her own well-being.

These two examples build both keys. That is, both show that encouragement can come from the most unexpected people. High intelligence, intact mental systems, education, brilliance—none of these are necessary to communicate love and care. These examples show the way people of apparent competence, achievement and health still need their spirits nourished and that they will take nourishment from anyone who is willing to offer it.

Everyone needs encouragement

Over the years I have watched (and even inquired of) a lot of people, both the highly accomplished and ordinary citizens, to learn how it is with their appetites for support and encouragement. I have found none who lack the hunger for appreciation and words of loving kindness that support them and their efforts, no matter who they are, how confident they look, how gorgeous, famous, wealthy or honored. The opposite is also true: those in food-spattered aprons, greasy handed mechanics, distant teenagers, tattooed gang member—all have the hunger. It is universal.

I have been told that the great opera singer, Luciano Pavoratti, carries a favorite positive newspaper clipping in his wallet. Before this most famous tenor in the world sings, he will read those words of appreciation to build his confidence and enhance his performance. He is not beyond needing to be inspired by the words of someone who speaks kindly of his work.

Most head for the exit

Failure to see this may account for what happens at every planned event where someone goes up front to announce, teach, speak, sing or entertain in some other way. After such events, whether it is a professor who lectures, a musician who performs, a pastor who expounds, or a docent who tour-guides, 99% of the audience promptly walks away without a word of personal appreciation. This happens no matter how good the presentation was. It is not a sign that the program was deficient. It is a sign that most people assume the one up front has all the confidence and assurance they will ever need or else they would not be doing what they are doing. Going back to Essential Key #1, the departing spectator assumes her comments aren't going to be valued, anyway.

When I was leading our staff devotions recently, before getting into my talk, I asked one group of eight employees around a table to come up afterward and say to me, *"Thank you for speaking to us today."* I wanted to teach a Care and Kindness lesson.

I made the request lightheartedly, but they did what I asked. Every one of them spoke the sentence of appreciation I'd suggested. Guess what! Even though it was arranged— and possibly not genuine from their hearts—it still made me feel good!

This is not a brand new discovery. We have known for ages that runners and performers of all kinds do better when surrounded by cheering crowds. Everybody does better when cheered. Write these truths in your heart. The list of potential targets for your encouragement is endless— the cashier at the 7-11, the car wash staff, the bus driver, banker, receptionist. You have what they need and they need what you have.

Essential Key #3: Care and Kindness, whether it is my smile, a word of thanks, a visit, or treating others fairly, builds hope and happiness in their hearts and opens them to God's love.

Hope lives in the human spirit from birth on. From earliest childhood, we are looking forward to new possibilities. We look for new opportunities, fresh experiences, higher plateaus to live on. Our hearts long for and look for security, love, and accomplishments. Whatever it is that we think might happen or is possible, we can call Hope. Such anticipation keeps us living, striving, working and waiting. Most human beings carry in their hearts a Hope for good things to come.

Ordinary life, with its unexpected and predictable harassments, struggles, setbacks and pitfalls, can injure, threaten, and even diminish the Hope in the human spirit. Abuse, poverty, sickness, burdens too heavy to carry, tiredness, threats, the lurking danger of terrorism, or the loss of loved ones, can damage and nearly kill Hope in some. A strong trust in (and continual focusing on) God's promises is one of the strongest antidotes to hold off the draining and destroying forces that attack our Hopefulness. God has implanted Hope rather solidly in the human heart but it can be wounded and shrunk by life experience. We say "Hope springs eternal in the human heart." But Hope is not invulnerable and needs replenishment almost every day.

Hope-building made easy

Good people, acting with Care and Kindness, help build and defend Hope. God depends on our loving kindness to nourish Hope in those around us. God's spirit flows through us. We are strengthening and restoring Hope every time we speak a word, or give a touch that reassures another. Such deeds send a message, announcing there is goodness in this world, not just meanness, selfishness and greed. Support and appreciation rebuild the discouraged, whose Hopes may be waning. Such acts tell the recipient there is goodness (which is Godness) in this world and helps them keep their Hopes alive.

Loving-kindness is so powerful that an ancient Proverb said, "Kind words bring life." Another says, "Kind words are like honey, sweet to the taste and good for your health."

These may be words of long ago, but the medical world still recognizes these truths. They know that the person's spirit must be cared for if the body is going to gain strength. We know that broken and wounded spirits, which are the result of everything, from loss of a job to the death of a loved one, can even cause bodies to break down and become ill. Conversely, happy and Hopeful souls do well in fighting diseases, injuries and other physical breakdowns.

Life is empty without hope

So every follower of Jesus must understand that he/she is not only the "light of the world" in an abstract sense, but that we are all deliverers of ingredients that bring God to people. When we bring God in the form of Care and Kindness, we are reinforcing Hope. Strengthened Hope is a necessary ingredient for positive living in a world that feels and looks oppressive unless God is seen nearby. God is seen and felt, even if not named, when we give tastes of God through Care and Kindness, compassion, love and encouragement. Concrete words and acts that show concern, interest, and consideration give a strong boost to God's promise to be present to us in every condition of life.

Christian Hope includes a passion for God's promise of life after death—the Easter promise. When we regularly sprinkle tastes of God through our intentional spirit-lifting behavior, we enable others to believe there is a good God who will never leave us or forsake us, in this life or the life to come. That is how important it is for ordinary people to be conscientious deliverers, day after day, of God's love, disguised as caring and concern.

Someone once said that our role in life is to "give birth to God", which we do with every large or small act of Care and Kindness we offer. Giving goodness gives nourishment and strength to the Hope in another's heart. His or her confidence, dreams and optimism about life are enlarged through simple acts of Care and Kindness.

> Kind words toward those you daily meet,
> Kind words and actions right,
> Will make this life of ours more sweet
> Turn darkness into light.
> **Isaac Watts**

Essential Key #4: Care and Kindness toward anyone is Care and Kindness to the Lord.

> I tell you the truth,
> whatever you did for one of the least
> of these brothers of mine,
> you did for me.
> **Matthew 25:40**

The substance of this essential key, and the words of Jesus on which it is based, is that the human race is incredibly valued by God. He equates care for any human being with care for the Lord Jesus Christ. This an amazing parity no other religion would ever make, that women and men are seen with love and value at the highest level conceivable.

The words of John 3:16 show the extent of God's value for His image bearers:

> God so loved the world
> that he gave his one and only son,
> that whoever believes in him shall not perish but
> have eternal life.
> **John 3:16**

If that is how much God loves the human race, we are obliged to see people as treasures to be valued, appreciated, encouraged, helped every way we are able.

The almighty God, whom we know in Jesus Christ, so personally identifies with each of us that Care and Kindness to anybody is felt by Him with thankfulness that His children are being cared for.

You can't love everybody

No one can love everybody or meet all the needs surrounding us. There are countless hurting people from whom we turn sadly away, either overwhelmed or incapacitated in some way. God understands our limitations. We contribute what we can. But to rush on through life with ears closed and eyes averted, as we seek our pleasant satisfactions, is a lifestyle unacceptable for followers of Jesus. I want to stand before Jesus wounded and weary from well-doing—not glowing with the satisfactions of a lifestyle of minimal pain. We cannot love everybody, but we can do something for many.

Essential Key #5: Care and Kindness is infectious. Others catch it and pass it on.

A Reader's Digest story years ago told of a man living in the middle of a dismal slum in a large city. One day something inspired him to prepare a window box with colorful flowers to hang on the front of his run-down apartment. Surprisingly, that spot of beauty set off a chain reaction. One after another, up and down the street, neighbors painted a door, planted some petunias, towed away broken-down vehicles, cut grass and pulled weeds. Soon that street was clean and attractive and quite a contrast to adjacent areas. Beauty had infected the residents—ignited by one man's flowers. They caught it and beauty spread.

A well-known expression claims that "one bad apple spoils the whole barrel". We know that is true, but the opposite is true also (although not for apples). One good deed inspires another. They are caught and multiplied. They travel like ripples on a pond, far beyond the initial splash.

Good deeds are catching

Freeway driving teaches the infection theory. Let a driver into the lane you are occupying when she puts on her turn signal and inches over. Seconds later, she will do the same for someone in front of her. Not only do they help each other, but each generous spirited person receives a surge of good feelings that blesses their entire system for many minutes to come. Good deeds are good for one's health.

> "When we see someone do a good deed…it elevates our view of human nature. That elevation can produce physical changes: the proverbial lump in the throat or tightness in the chest. It also triggers altruism. Once elevated, people often feel inspired to do their own good deeds" —Jon Haidt
> Quoted in the **Los Angeles Times**, July 22, 2002

A research scheme used the coin return on a pay telephone to test human behavior. The researchers would sometimes place several dimes and quarters in the coin return. They discovered that when a person came by and found the change, he would usually respond helpfully to a staged dilemma nearby where a woman had dropped her bag of groceries. Those who checked the coin return and found it empty were far less likely to help the woman in distress. Good fortune, received in the form of a few quarters and dimes, affected the recipient so positively that he would act kindly to another.

"Good can be as communicable and catching as evil, and that is where kindness and compassion come in to play," says Norman Corwin. "So long as conscionable and caring people are around, so long as they are not muted or exiled, so long as they remain alert in thought and action, there is a chance for contagions of the right stuff…"

Nothing better than a smile

Another example pointing to the contagiousness of Care and Kindness is the smile. It is nearly impossible to refrain from smiling when someone smiles at you.

An unknown poet has put this truth into poetic form:

> When someone smiled at me today,
> I started smiling too,
> I passed around the corner,
> and someone saw my grin.
> When he smiled, I realized
> I'd passed it on to him.
> I thought about that smile;
> Then I realized its worth.
> A single smile just like mine
> Could travel, 'round the earth.
> So if you feel a smile begin,
> Don't leave it undetected.
> Let's start an epidemic quick
> And get the world infected.

These are the Five Keys. Now prayerfully and thoughtfully promise to make them a part of your campaign to help make this world a better place. We improve life on earth by shedding God's light through our personalities into the world around us. Each little bit we contribute helps bring heaven to earth.

Discussion questions for Chapter 2 are on pages 225–227

※ ※ ※ ※ ※ ※ ※

Kindness Example

Dayna Butterbaugh, recently diagnosed with breast cancer, and in the middle of high-level treatment, was in a beauty supply store. A stranger walked in and effusively praised Dayna's beautiful head of hair. *"It's a wig. It's a wig,"* shouted the shop owner.

Naturally, the customer inquired about the circumstances. *"Chemo! Chemo!"* shouted the woman shopkeeper. This turned the encounter serious as the admiring woman realized the nature of what she was now part of. Surprisingly, the stranger and Dayna connected on the spiritual level, while the shopkeeper observed in bewilderment.

Her new friend strongly encouraged Dayna to purchase the wig. *"It is perfect for you,"* she said. But the $200.00 price tag was too much for Dayna without first making a phone call to her husband. She called him and he readily agreed she should buy it.

As Dayna moved toward the cash register, the stranger was already leaving. They embraced and Dayna received a promise of prayer.

At the cash register the shopkeeper said to Dayna, *"That was a very nice woman."* *"Yes, she was,"* agreed Dayna, opening her purse. *"No, I mean she was VERY nice, she just paid for your wig,"* the smiling shopkeeper gushed, *"I have never seen anything like this."* Then they both cried.

Reflection: Three people were blessed by this act of kindness. Then scores more, as the story is told. The ripples of kindness keep going out indefinitely.

※ ※ ※ ※ ※ ※ ※

ഉ൴ഉ൴ഉ൴ഉ൴ഉ൴ഉ൴ഉ൴

Kindness Example

Adella Cooper was a giant of Care and Kindness. In addition to her own daughter, she raised her sister's children after their mother died. Later, she and her husband, Fred, took in another dying woman's kids and cared for them also as their own until they matured and took flight.

In the middle of it all, Adella became deathly ill and her life hung in the balance. One of her special visitors was Arvella Schuller. What Arvella said, Adella testified later, literally turned her around and saved her life. Arvella whispered, *"God loves you totally and completely in every cell of your body."* The power of those promises sparked her recovery.

Reflection: A carefully chosen sentence, crafted with love, can lift a weakened spirit. Her hope renewed and revived her body.

ഉ൴ഉ൴ഉ൴ഉ൴ഉ൴ഉ൴ഉ൴

ৡৡৡৡৡৡৡ

Kindness Example

Sue Beck made a pastoral call on Isabel McKarnan at the care facility in which she resides. While visiting, Sue noticed Isabel's clock was standing still. So Sue asked the administrator if there were fresh batteries available. She was told the clock was broken, rather than needing batteries.

When Sue went back and took a closer look at the clock, she found there were no batteries in it at all. So Sue bought a package of AAAs , installed them, and the "tick-tock" began moving again.

Reflection: Caring about the simple needs in another's life is where loving kindness begins. Often the major issues are covered by those responsible, but the small conveniences and discomforts may be overlooked. That is what friends are for, I believe.

ৡৡৡৡৡৡৡ

-3-

Where Is God In All This?

"The Lord is weeping with you," I said. For the first time in many weeks of meeting together, she raised her head and looked at me as if I had touched something. Little, or nothing, had seemed to make any difference to her in all our previous weeks together since her six year old son had been killed by a car while riding his bike. *"How can you say that?"* she asked.

To answer her, I drew on Jesus words, paraphrasing a little: *"Inasmuch as it happens to the least of my little ones, it happens to me."* I then assured the young mother that Jesus totally identifies with her in the death of her little boy. *"It is like it happened to him,"* I insisted strongly.

It seemed like she showed visible signs of strengthening from this new truth. The thought of Jesus hurting with her appeared to make a noticeable difference.

Compassion is God's nature

Today, I would say a little more. I would add that it is the very nature of God to weep with us in our heartbreak. One of the most repeated descriptions of God is that he is compassionate. Compassion means to "feel with". So today I enrich my teaching that Jesus weeps with us by stressing that this is the very nature of God.

The Lord is gracious
And compassionate,
slow to anger
and rich in love.
The Lord is good to all;
He has compassion
On all he has made.
Psalm 145:8–9

This, then, is the picture: God is touched by the cries, groans and tears of his people. So, too, we are called to be responsive to the plight of those around us.

Compassion insists that we reach out to those in need and do whatever we can to free them from despair and feelings of hopelessness. We must find ways to support and encourage those in any kind of bondage and heartache that life might bring.

The only thing that counts is faith
expressing itself through love.
Gal. 5:6b

Compassion is in our nature, too

We are created in the image of God. Compassion is part of our nature. Therefore, compassion, as we see it defining God, is also part of who we are. Compassion is a central quality in the essence of human beings—part of being a true human being. Failure to actively express compassion, to ignore that which we are born with, is to squelch, ignore, and anesthetize a central quality of the human spirit, the God quality called compassion.

This kind of compassion is usually appreciated by those in pain. What more could one hope for than someone sharing your distress so personally? And God does exactly that.

Right from the beginning, in Genesis 6:6, there is a window showing the heart of God. These words follow the cataclysmic Fall of our first parents, Adam and Eve. It says:

> The Lord was grieved...
> and his heart was filled with pain.
> **Genesis 6:6**

God here is portrayed as touched by the circumstances of early people. God is brokenhearted over what had become of humanity. The world was broken by sin and God is anguished over that. This is a resounding surprise to many of us. Instead of a powerful, distant, controlling Creator, we see a personally invested Lord whose peace is disturbed and upset. God, we are being shown, cares personally about human conditions.

A child's tears touch God

Later, in the life of Abraham, there is another telling drama. His servant-wife, Hagar, and her child, Ishmael, are banished from the family camp due to her insubordination. They are sent to die in the wilderness. What happens? The account says God heard the boy crying! Then the angel of God called to Hagar:

> Do not be afraid!
> God has heard the boy crying as he lies there...
> Lift the boy up and take him by the hand...
> **Genesis 21:17**

Then God opened Hagar's eyes—she saw a well of water and their lives were saved. The Almighty God hears a child crying and responds with aid and provisions to save his life! A growing impression is building of a God who is compassionate toward hurting people. The Creator is caring, and moved by the anguish of human beings. This is Divinity of a revolutionary kind. A personally touchable

God is being revealed to us. Such a picture can radically affect how we think of, and relate to, this God.

Decades later the Chosen People are enslaved by the Pharaohs of Egypt. After several generations of slavery we read:

> The Israelites groaned in their slavery
> and cried out,
> and their cry for help...went up to God.
> God heard their groaning
> and he remembered his covenant...
> So, God looked on them and was concerned...
> **Exodus 2:23**

This is a world-changing event. Their groaning, heard by God, leads to the great Exodus! They are released from centuries of slavery because they groaned and cried to God, and God was touched and moved to the point of freeing them. Here is God exhibiting the essence of compassion.

The Exodus from slavery is celebrated later in Moses' words:

> Then we cried out to the Lord,
> the God of our Fathers,
> and the Lord heard our voice
> and saw our misery, toil and oppression.
> So the Lord brought us out of Egypt
> with a mighty hand and an outstretched arm.
> **Deuteronomy 26:7**

This is a clear picture of a God who feels the pain of his children and cares for them in tangible ways. The Psalms are filled with evidence and celebration of God's compassion.

> The Lord has heard my weeping.
> The Lord has heard my cry for mercy;
> the Lord accepts my prayer
> **Psalm 6:8–9**

They were hungry and thirsty,
and their lives ebbed away.
Then they cried out to the Lord in their trouble
and he delivered them from their distress.
Psalm 107:5

The eyes of the Lord are on the righteous
and his ears are attentive to their cry…
The righteous cry out.
And the Lord hears them;
he delivers them from their troubles.
The Lord is close to the broken hearted
and saves those who are crushed in spirit.
Psalm 34:15–18

The essence of God, as pictured in these Psalms and so strikingly in Psalm 145 at the beginning of this chapter, is God's compassionate, caring, responsive nature.

Because he loves me, says the Lord,
I will rescue him;
I will protect him,
for he acknowledges my name.
He will call on me, and I will answer him
I will be with him in trouble,
I will deliver him and honor him…
Psalm 91:14–16

Tears again

Let's look at one more example that shows that the very essence of God is compassion, feeling for his people, and that God is touched by their cries and prayers. This is the story of King Hezekiah, who has been told by the prophet Isaiah that he is going to die of his illness. Here is how the king responds to this bad news:

Hezekiah turned his face to the wall
and prayed to the Lord…
And Hezekiah wept bitterly…

before Isaiah had left the middle court,
the word of the Lord came to him:
Go back and tell Hezekiah,
the leader of my people ...
I have heard your prayer
and seen your tears;
I will heal you...
II Kings 20:2–5

Notice it was not just his prayer but his tears that moved God. Another vital portrayal of the compassion in the heart of God. When heartache and disappointment strike us, this is how we can picture God.

God's love brings us Jesus

The birth, life, death and resurrection of Jesus are all part of the same phenomenon. The Creator's anguish over an aimless, lost, hopeless human race turned into the Plan of Salvation. The caring, broken-hearted God comes to his people in Jesus. Here is infinite compassion made tangible, effective, and world saving. Care and Kindness of the ultimate kind, right out of the heart of God, defines the entire life and person of Jesus. The incarnation of Jesus is compassion made tangible, visible, incarnate.

The inspiring and surprising picture of God we have been looking at proclaims His nature with stunning clarity. The compassion that defines God so convincingly teaches us two vital and life-changing lessons.

(1) We can give thanks for God's personal intimate care for each of us when we are wounded by life, in any way. God is not distant, apathetically allowing or planning such breakdowns and heartaches. God is wounded, too, and weeping with us.

(2) The second lesson is essential for our Care and Kindness mission. It is that we who are created in the

image of God are likewise to be actively brokenhearted over the grievances and failures, the heartaches and anguish, of people in this world. Deeply touched, as God is, we must live actively, expressing care and compassion every way we can:

> He has shown you...what is good....
> To act justly, and to love mercy
> and to walk humbly with your God
> **Micah 6:8**

> Since God chose you to be
> the holy people whom he loves,
> you must clothe yourselves with compassion,
> kindness, humility, gentleness and patience...
> **Col. 3:12**

My pain is shallow

A short time ago, I had the responsibility to officiate at the funeral for two little children, Cody, age 5, and Courtney, age 3. They had been murdered by their father. Tragedies seldom get worse than this. I did my best to support their surviving mother, while calling for the death penalty for the murderer. Later, I realized how shallow my anguish really was compared to the enormity of the horrific crime. My capacity for anguish was so primitive and elementary compared to what the horrific evilness deserved. If I felt fully what the loss deserved, there would be nothing left of me.

God's pain is limitless

It was then that I thought of how God must be hurt beyond our power to imagine. God hurt over Cody and Courtney appropriately, which means his pain was infinitely deep and long. Mine fell way short of what this horror deserved.

God hurts over Cody and Courtney to the maximum possible. There is comfort in that. We do the best we can to care as deeply as our limited spirits are able. God cares without limit.

In the example of Hagar and Ishmael, God heard and responded to the cries of the child, even when they were not intentionally directed to Him. So too, we must hear the unspoken and the inaudible cries and groans of those around us, as well as the visible and audible. We must see those in need of support, encouragement and appreciation and give to them as best we can in small, simple, or majestic and profound ways. Our lives must, God-like, express feeling for others through and through.

Jesus put it this way:

> I was hungry
> and you gave me something to eat,
> I was thirsty
> and you gave me something to drink,
> I was a stranger
> and you invited me in,
> I was sick
> and you looked after me,
> I was in prison
> and you came to visit me.
> **Matthew 25:35–36**

Some caring folks do truly, God-like, so closely identify with others that their hearts ache for them and with them. The capacity for this differs from one person to another. There are those who quickly, naturally and deeply, connect with those in struggles, loss or tragedy. Their tears readily flow, their stomachs ache, their sleep is disturbed on behalf of a friend or even a stranger.

Is it necessary that *"I feel your pain"*?

It is advantageous and natural to know personally the emotional side effects of life's blows and blasts; that is, to know how they feel. Empathy—the capacity to project another's feelings into your own in order to know what they are going through—is only possible in those who are capable of naming feelings in themselves. If you claim or name no feelings, you are not one who has the ability to empathize.

Some lack feelings

It may sound strong to claim or honestly experience losses and crashes with no distress, or discomfort. For example, those who always say, *"No, I am not sad"* after a dear one dies may be speaking honestly. They who say, *"No, I am not afraid"* when there is a dangerous predator nearby may be true to their feelings or lack of them. But what they do not realize is that they are handicapped! They are not equipped to express sympathy to another or feel empathy toward them if they do not personally know the feeling of sadness or fear. To lack feelings in obviously emotional situations is to have something closed down that should be functioning. Healthy people feel sadness and fear. This equips them to understand what others are feeling in related or similar crises.

You can feel more

Caring people can enlarge their repertoire of feelings by thoughtfully working at identifying the feelings within themselves that they are not aware of. For instance, the death of a loved one is, by definition, nearly always sad. When it happens to anyone, there is sadness inside them somewhere. Those who lose a loved one can be enabled to begin naming their sorrow and even to begin feeling it when it is not immediately available to their consciousness for some reason. This can often be enhanced by a thoughtful friend working with them. Little by little, they may get in touch and begin to be able to name their feelings. This is a helpful part of the healing process. Lively feelings are part of being God-like.

Can I really care if I do not feel another's pain?

If I find myself face to face with the brokenhearted, but my feelings fail to engage, am I a suitable care-giver? When appropriate words come out of my mouth but internally I am dead or detached, should my care-credentials be revoked? Must I feel another's fear, sadness, discouragement, in order to "show up" and effectively speak or pray with them?

Use your head

Care and Kindness can be delivered, even by those who feel little. Need is often obvious. We can see need. It is visibly there and we can choose to help. No feelings are necessary to know someone with a bleeding wound needs assistance. Every intelligent soul knows there is sorrow when a mother's child dies. One's emotional system may be lacking in sensitivity, but our mental processes can take over and lead us into places where we can show loving kindness in some tangible way. We can see it and know it, even if we do not feel it. The need is everywhere and it is usually quite conspicuous.

Care is more than feelings

Followers of Jesus know they are God's army of helpers, placed in this world to help make it better, wherever possible. Therefore, even those with very little ability to identify or name their feelings can be giants in delivery of Care and Kindness. They must just use their heads more than their hearts. They will see pain, and act to restore and comfort, even when they feel little. Care must be more than feelings. Helpful people need to be very thoughtful and even analytic as they enter the lives of hurting folks. And often, good thinking does not coexist with feeling strongly. When the brain engages, emotions may, at least temporarily, recede. Intense feelings can incapacitate keen thinking for a time. William James said, "We are an ocean of emotion and a speck of reason." Keeping that speck of reason engaged is crucial so that the ocean of emotion is controlled and the correct action is delivered.

When I, as a Pastor, am at the bedside of someone going through an agonizing ordeal, I feel little. My brain is working overtime as I see the difficult struggle. I am thinking—shall I stand or sit? Shall I stay briefly or try to engage the man in conversation? What shall I say? How should I pray? Shall I touch him or not? Shall I pray for the man in the next bed also? What is his wife's name? All these questions and others are zipping through my mind, allowing for little palpable awareness of compassionate feelings, empathy or sympathy. At the same time, my busy brain is aware of and tuned to the fears, apprehension, gratification or upset-ness he in the bed is likely to be experiencing. In reality, I probably function more effectively when I am cooler emotionally.

Care requires thought

True care zeroes in on what the person needs. That takes thought: assessing what may be helpful. Surging emotions can short-circuit finding the right way to connect. Doing the right thing may require cool, well-focused, thoughtful action. Understanding that another is upset or grieved is essential, but having their feelings is not necessary.

So the answer is "no". We are not disqualified for care on the basis of failing to truly resonate to someone else's personal anguish. Feeling another's pain, or being emotionally affected, because someone else is in anguish, is not a necessary requirement for care. It is more important to do the right thing than feel the right feelings. But being a feeling person is healthier than to be unfeeling. When we do not feel, we are not in touch with reality because the presence of feelings is a known fact, even if we cannot name them.

Example #1 — Caring, when you don't care

Sue says: *"Dusty, our 18-year-old Siamese cat, died yesterday. Well, actually, we had to have her put to sleep. It was so hard to do."*

Care Person (who, incidentally, is both allergic to cats and dislikes them in general) says:
"Oooh, how sad. I'm sure after such a long life, it's like losing a family member."

The Care Person feels no sorrow about the demise of the cat. This is a caring act from his head—an empathic sentence based on his awareness that this is sad for Sue. He expresses understanding and acceptance, even though his feelings are totally numb or indifferent about the death of the cat. Most importantly, his words are helpful.

One other slant on this: To survive very long as a warm caring person, some distancing is necessary. With little or no capacity to stay somewhat at arm's length, the courage to continue will soon diminish. And the other probability is what is called burnout. Then the care person may continue to "show up" in the world of hurting people but slowly be reduced to robotic-like involvement—a sort of "going through the motions" kind of living and caring. With experience, appropriate detachment happens almost naturally and thereby the caring friends are insulated from burnout. God has unlimited capacity for compassion. We do not.

Example #2 — Caring When Your Mind is Busy

The Pastor has been called to the home of Mr. J., who is under Hospice care and extremely weak. The son, who greets him at the door, says, *"We're still praying for a miracle."*

The Pastor is now confronted with the need to think consciously about how to conduct his ministry to this family, a family he knows well and loves. From the moment he is greeted at the door until he leaves, the Pastor is thinking hard, assessing the situation, choosing his sentences of prayer carefully, mindful of those present, as well as the sick man.

The Pastor is not sad or feeling heartache—he is endeavoring to do a sensitive task as best he can. His feelings are disengaged. His care is thoughtfully being worked out in order to do the best pastoral care he is able to produce.

When feelings don't make sense

Truthfully, it is impossible to feel another's pain precisely. We can be touched by her distress; or his tears can trigger ours. But when we do feel very strongly in the presence of someone else's heartache, it sometimes means the situation is stirring up old distress of our own. Occasionally there may be "unfinished business" surfacing, either from past history or from fears or hurts that we still carry.

I recall having a rush of tearfulness one evening when I got out of my car in the parking lot of a funeral home. Those I came to pay my respects to were not dear friends and I hardly knew the deceased. Still I was crying. I realized that the surroundings were very much like the Mortuary where my brother, Woody, had been taken when he died. Others might have seen me as caring deeply for the family I was visiting, but my tears were for my own loss of a year earlier, triggered by the environment of sadness.

Another's anguish is always unique.

We may have had a similar experience to someone else, but it is impossible to know *exactly* how it is with him or her. To say, *"I understand,"* therefore, rarely finds a receptive ear and is seldom accurate; it is usually better left unsaid.

A parent who has lost a child may say, *"I know how you feel"* to a mother who is now in such pain and her words are credible and helpful. But each still hurts in her own way, never exactly the same.

How about when your mind wanders?

The helping person gives what the wounded needs, regardless of her own inner turmoil, preoccupation, weariness, or whatever else is percolating inside her. She may focus intently on the other's words, make attentive eye-contact, gently hold her hand, say and pray tender words of hope and assurance. *(Her mind–the care-giver's– may, however, be flitting to her illegally parked car, an appointment for which she is already late, and the likelihood that she will need to skip lunch.)*

Nevertheless, the recipient of her care is being blessed by this love. It is doubtful the caregiver's inevitable inner distractions diminish the goodness of the care very much. Her mind, as well as her heart, may be elsewhere, but her action is healing and spirit calming for the hurting one.

Don't confuse this with apathy

On the other hand, to totally lack such feelings of compassion is more of a worry. If we feel no concern, we should wonder where the compassion of Godliness is buried or how it has become extinguished in ourselves. When we lack feelings we are apathetic.

Apathy means to lack feelings of empathy or sympathy. I have met a few who lack feelings. Often a family history turns up intense and serious emotional trauma in early life. Childhood for some was so disturbing that they turned their feelings off permanently. They survive, sometimes quite well, with no conscious capacity for empathy or sympathy. Such a condition calls for them to work more diligently and earnestly to show compassion, even though they may not feel it.

Total identification of one to another is exclusively God's capacity. God, in Jesus, knows our pain and our joys with a perfect correlation.

When Jesus said, "Inasmuch as you do it to one of the least of these my little ones, you do it to me," he was making it

clear about where he is for us. When we hurt, he hurts.
When joy lifts us, he is lifted, too.

Keep compassion central

We understand now that we are called to keep compassion
central in our lives. God-like, we are those who must
respond to those in need. It isn't always that easy. No one
enjoys distressing emotions. But to feel sad, worried,
brokenhearted, upset and even angry over the plight of a
friend or a stranger is a necessary result of being a kind and
compassionate person. Strong feelings are not a weakness
or a shameful flaw to be hid or covered. Such emotions are
part of God living in us. Feeling tender, angry, or sad is
evidence of the Spirit of God in us. It is like God to be
caring and moved by the brokenness and struggles of
others.

Cards and casseroles

We, as God's helpers, feel for others, more or less. We
cannot feel very deeply another's anguish, or very long.
But in helping, actions speak louder than feelings. It's
"showing up" and doing what we can, saying and doing
what we believe helpful, that counts. Our caring actions
are more life-giving than the feelings of empathy or
sympathy. It's our cards and casseroles, hugs and
handshakes, smiles and tears, walking with and sitting with,
our prayers and promises to pray that really make a
difference in helping the hurting.

And they help a lot!

The Christian writer Anne La Mott remembers her Pastor's
words as a touching reminder of our central business on
planet earth:

"Our preacher Veronica said recently that this is life's nature: that lives and hearts get broken— those of people we love; those of people we'll never meet. She said that the world sometimes feels like the waiting room of the emergency ward and that we, who are more or less okay for now, need to take the tenderest possible care of the more wounded people in the waiting room until The Healer comes. You sit with people, she said, you bring them juice and graham crackers."
Traveling Mercies, Anne La Mott, p106

Avoid doing too much

These teachings are aimed at those who have big hearts and strong caring intentions but who, as human beings, can easily be pulled in further than they intended, or further than they can handle. Doing too much is the number one reason loving people pull back and drop away from their desire to be consistent deliverers of Care and Kindness.

Fortunately, the human capacity for empathy is not enormous. We can feel for others, but it doesn't often go very deep. Or, if it is deep, it seldom lasts very long. When we ponder the heart of God, we are led to see God as experiencing our pain, the anguish of humanity, infinitely. Ours is shallow and brief. Nicholas Wolterstorff reasons in his book, **Lament for a Son,** that God's face is so full of pain from caring for the human race that we cannot bear to look at it.

Denial is a big help

For us to be wracked by pain, when disaster, tragedy, failures and heartaches of international or personal proportions come into our vision, is not a huge concern.

It is seldom incapacitating. God has equipped us with shut-off valves that keep our compassion, empathy and sympathy brief and relatively shallow. Our humanness includes this capacity to hurt for others. But, it is limited. God has also given us extremely agile denial valves that work well. Seldom are we disabled by another's tragedy. For this we can be grateful to God, while also humbly acknowledging our limitations.

Learn to set limits

If, however, "Harvey", becomes emotionally upset each time he gets involved in someone's grief or terminal illness, he may grow cautious about calling and caring. A natural reflex to avoid distress may trigger avoidance. A healthy minded person deliberately avoids unnecessary pain, rather than moving voluntarily toward it. Here is where a good soul, such as Harvey, may profit from a little training, to help him care without such adverse consequences. Otherwise, he may stop showing up.

A little training helps

Training does not mean something so daunting as a college course or advanced degree. Amateurs need small doses of instruction. That is why we started the Conference on Care and Kindness at The Crystal Cathedral. Our workshops tell about caring for life's challenges, such as Alzheimer's, Suicide, Depression, or Death of a Child. Other workshops are like Debbie Hutchinson's talk on the simple art of setting limits. When caring folks see and set boundaries, they are better equipped to continue, instead of drifting away.

My own mini-lecture is entitled "**Care for them, but you do not have to adopt them.**" My point is that a caring word or a few minutes of listening are tremendously appreciated, but after reaching out to a wounded soul, it is okay to bid farewell without a feeling of obligation to take the person out for lunch or to call every day after that.

That is why training can help Harvey—both brightening the lives of others and garnering blessings for himself. Our goal in this project is to motivate Harvey and keep him playing on the Care and Kindness "1st Team".

We want Harvey to be realistic in his good-heartedness so his spirit is not depleted by the loving kindness he spreads around. We want him to continue as an energetic amateur the rest of his life. We do not want him to "grow weary in well-doing" (St Paul's words) and phase out of his well-intentioned efforts because of feeling exhausted.

The Harveys who are motivated by love and commitment (amateurs) need at times to listen to the professionals. Professionals have been taught and they have learned what it means to give thoughtful attention to setting limits. Likewise, caregivers who can stay in the race must recognize realistic boundaries on what they attempt to accomplish. They must sensibly ration their God-given energies. Then they will endure.

C.S. Lewis shares a precaution caring folks must be aware of. He reminds us of the hurts involved, but the greater danger of avoiding them:

> "To love at all is to be vulnerable. Love anything and your heart will certainly be wrung and possibly broken. If you want to make sure of keeping it intact, you must give your heart to no one…Wrap it up carefully with hobbies and little luxuries; avoid all entanglements, lock it up safe in the casket or coffin of your selfishness. But in that casket—safe, dark, motionless, airless—it

will change. It will not be broken; it will become unbreakable, impenetrable, irredeemable..."
The Four Loves, C.S. Lewis, 1960.

The following parable of The Cocoon teaches that we should not be too quick to intrude on people's struggles when they are caught in tight squeezes. God will work the healing. Stand by! Pray. Have faith. Wait. God's way will work.

The Cocoon

A man came home one day and discovered a moth cocoon near his door. He became curious and wanted to watch the moth emerge, so he took it inside and put it in a warm place. Soon the moth began to break through the top of the cocoon. It made a small hole and then seemed to be unable to free itself further. As the man watched, he became impatient and worried because the moth seemed to be making no progress in breaking free. In an effort to be helpful, the man cut a larger hole in the top of the cocoon and the moth emerged soon after.

To the man's dismay, the moth came out with a large, bloated body and small undeveloped wings. It couldn't fly and had great difficulty managing its unwieldy body.

Sometime later, the man talked to his friend, who taught biology, and told him about his anemic moth. What he was told by the biologist was enlightening. In his efforts to make it easier for the moth, the man hadn't realized the central role that a seemingly insurmountable effort played in the emergence of a healthy, viable adult moth. He didn't know that it was essential for the moth to struggle. It was the process of squeezing through the hole that forced the liquid in the moth's body out into its wings. Under normal circumstances, by the time an adult moth has struggled through the small hole in the cocoon, its body is smaller and its wings are large enough to support it. Effort and struggle comprise the key to healthy development for the adult moth.

God doesn't make it easy

By trying to make the entrance into this world easier for the moth, a form of "fixing", he deprived it of an essential step in its development. When we apply this example to human life, this does not mean that people are necessarily assigned heartaches and catastrophes or other tough times as essential to their becoming what they are intended to become, as far as we know. However, struggles are full of potential for deepening, enriching, and stretching the mind, the heart, and the soul when we are the recipients of such difficulties.

I love the parable of the Cocoon because it helps me understand where God is. In all our heartaches, in all our hurts, when we wish and think God should rescue us, but he doesn't, this helps. In the struggles we have to go through, God is there with us, strengthening us, inspiring us, hurting with us. God is walking alongside as we emerge into something even better than we were before. And we "show up" as God's agents—not to rescue, but to be present as they hurt, stretch, fight and struggle. And they become, as many of you have, far more than they were before. With God's help, and the presence of loving people, the metamorphosis of suffering can be deeply positive, even though slow and painful.

Where is God in all this?

The compassion of God is such a powerful balm for the weary and wounded. Reminding the hurting of God's incredible identification with them is itself a gift of healing. Accepting the call and the responsibility to endeavor to let the compassion God has planted in us live and act is an enormous accomplishment and a part of proper living.

Like in all of life, we do what we can, intelligently finding balance somewhere in the middle between too little and too much. Too little is usually wrong or a symptom of something broken. Too much is sometimes wrong-spirited and grandiose; too much wears people out and sends them to less worthy pastimes instead.

Balance means doing what we can without neglecting other parts of life. When confronted with needs that would force us beyond our necessary boundaries, we entrust those needs to God and then leave it for others to step forward in our place.

Discussion questions for Chapter 3 are on pages 228–231.

ശ്ക്ക്ക്ക്ക്ക

Kindness Example

Sol Nunez told how he once shared his painful, emotional wound with a friend. *"She began to cry,"* he said. *"Nobody ever cried for my pain before,"* explained Sol. *"Her tears healed me a lot more than if she had read many Bible verses with me or even if she just prayed. It made me feel she understood what I was feeling and that my response was acceptable."*

Reflection: Too often we try to stop people from crying. We respond as if tears are a sign we have gone beyond an appropriate boundary. So we back off or grab a box of tissues to dry the water up as quickly as possible.

Tears are a gift of God. When they flow, toxins are emptying out and well-being is enhanced. They express our feelings powerfully in ways mere words cannot. Words often conceal—tears are mostly honest. In Biblical times, families would bring in gifted weepers to prime the pump of tears in the others who were present. They would stand and wail, causing others to weep. Tears were recognized as needed and appropriate—not as an unwanted or embarrassing bother.

So Sol Nunez recognized the rare gift he received when his friend wept with him. Her tears gave him permission to cry more. Plus her tears spoke deeply of her empathy and compassion for him. Her tears were a profound message of Care and Kindness too rare in our very verbal world.

ശ്ക്ക്ക്ക്ക്ക

⧏⧏⧏⧏⧏⧏⧏

Kindness Example

Colorado Rancher Vic Winter has a lot of work to do every day of the year. Nevertheless, he holds a quiet resolution to which he has stayed true for decades: he allows two hours daily to be available to help others. It is time when he is interruptible. He will drop everything to lend a hand or whatever he can offer for someone's need.

Reflection: Time is like a blank check to Vic's surrounding neighbors, friends and family. They may cash it in as they wish and he will honor it.

Behind such an offer lies a creative, generous-spirited heart. Cowboy Vic wants to be known as an interruptible man.

⧏⧏⧏⧏⧏⧏⧏

Kindness Example

On Monday morning, the day after Easter Sunday, I was on the grounds of The Crystal Cathedral at 7:00 o'clock. I was hoping to buy some of the plants that had been used to decorate the church for Easter. Besides the plants that were for sale, there were also hundreds of Easter Lilies set out on the plaza that were available free of charge.

There among the Easter Lilies, I spotted Ofelia Miller. She was loading her car with the flowers. She explained she was taking them to the graves near where her sister was buried at Westminster Cemetery. *"There is never a flower on any of them,"* Ofelia said. *"I decorate them a little at Easter and Christmas with our Crystal Cathedral leftovers."*

Further conversation uncovered that Ofelia has been offering this kindness since 1991.

Reflection: The best kind of care is that which costs you something and is secret. It took effort and energy to do what Ofelia was doing. She had to get out of bed early and drive to the church before the flowers were all gone. Plus, she did it in total secrecy. It was in no way motivated by what others might think because no one else knew about it. Except the smiling Jesus.

ৡৢৡৢৡৢৡৢৡৢ

-4-

Just Show Up

All different levels of need surround us. Everyone we meet is needy, so let us turn our attention to ways that we can show care everywhere as we develop the campaign of Care and Kindness. The more common thought, when the challenge "to care" is brought up, is concern for those who are seriously ill, in deep grief, or going through an unusually painful difficulty. I want to cut to the core of this basic issue by emphasizing the need to take action; to show loving kindness to the severely distressed—more than merely feeling concern for them.

The Mayor showed up

Former New York City Mayor Rudy Guiliani scored major goodwill points in the aftermath of the 9/11 tragedy. If you analyze what he did that was so powerfully appreciated by New Yorkers and the entire nation, you are not likely to point to an idea he developed, a sentence he uttered, or any speech he made. What he did was that he "showed up". He was there. He was present. He was close by the scene of disaster and he was visible. He left his office and avoided the TV studios in order to be a conspicuous presence where the hurt was.

In 1996, my book **90 % of Helping is Just Showing Up** arrived on the scene. The title became the theme of our Care and Kindness Conference, now held annually at The

Crystal Cathedral. The reason that people latched on to the "showing up" idea was its relevance for promoting lives and behaviors of Care and Kindness. This idea sweeps away one of the chronic reasons people stay at arms length from people in need: they fall back from those in distress because they think helping depends on being knowledgeable, articulate, and informed about the issue being faced. To help, most believe, demands knowing how to speak words that make things better for the one to whom they are talking. Some assume they need to know a raft of Bible texts or to be able to pray articulately. I have heard scores of times the excuse, *"Oh, I wouldn't know what to say,"* as a reason for staying away.

No excuses left

The **"90% is showing up"** maxim removes that excuse or misunderstanding. This "showing up" idea claims that when folks are hurting, help is not a matter of speaking excellently or "knowing what to say". Helping is a matter of coming to the person with concern in your heart. Your arrival with an awareness of hurt and need transmits a powerfully supportive message. It speaks more clearly than spoken syllables or timeless Bible verses. Being present to a concerned or struggling soul is in its own way a wonderful balm, a healing influence.

> When Natalie Dotson died after a long illness, her neighbors knocked on the door to extend their condolences to Harry, her husband. They explained that they had not come over during Natalie's illness because *"we didn't want to tire her and we knew there were so many others helping her."* Notice, however, that they deprived Natalie of the care and concern they could have offered—ostensibly because of some other things

they assumed were happening. In the cause of staying comfortable, any rationalization seems to work. They were not fair to Natalie, even if they supposed they were staying away for adequate reasons. One can guess that the real reason for not showing up was a feeling of fear, inadequacy or helplessness. But in reality, all they had to do was "show up." There was nothing to fear, no reason to stay away.

Peter Breedveld, an old friend of mine, reflects on this in his autobiography:

> A young man in his congregation had been killed by a hit-and-run drunk driver. "I immediately went to the bereaved family to offer help and comfort. Being a young student pastor, this was a traumatic experience for me—my first encounter with death. I read a portion of Scripture to them and offered a short prayer. The words stuck in my throat and after a minute, I just sat there and wept with the family. I was very self-conscious about my inability to speak words of comfort. I had yet to learn that just being there as a pastor, saying a short prayer and sharing in their grief meant more than all the words I could utter." **Changing,** by Peter Breedveld, p. 53. Essence Publishing, 2003

It is simple

This "just show up" theme fuels our efforts to motivate people to respond to those around them in a way anyone is capable of doing. The intention to motivate Care and Kindness receives an enormous boost when we realize caring is not the exclusive domain of experts, professionals, or the unusually gifted or trained. We must persuade the caring community of the simplicity of caring behavior. As we do that, we will strengthen and energize God's people to go way beyond the current level of daily acts of Care and Kindness.

Anne Lamott in **Traveling Mercies** writes about a small drama involving her young son.

> He was too small to make a swim he badly wanted to take part in and almost perished trying before he was rescued. Sam was grievously disappointed but he was very brave. I was desperate to fix him, fix the situation, make everything happy again, and then I remembered this basic religious principle: that God isn't there to take away our suffering or our pain but to fill it with his or her presence. So I prayed for the health simply to enter Sam's disappointment and keep him company. **p.241.**

The key words here are "keep him company." That idea gets at the heart of the "showing up" maxim. People are helped by the caring presence of others. It is not their words, usually, or a solution they can come up with. No, it is "being with" in a compassionate way. This can be relatively wordless, sometimes. Almost always, "being with" is in place of fixing the problem or restoring the loss. Presence is a powerful healing force available to all.

In another scene in **The Secret Life of Bees,** the young lady says,

> "I sat up, feeling like my body weighed two hundred pounds. Like somebody had backed the cement truck up to the honey house, swung the pipe over my chest, and started pouring…"

Then she adds this, referring to an imaginary Mary (the Mother of Jesus):

> "The only thing I wanted was for her to understand. Somebody to let out a big sigh and say, 'You poor thing, I know how you feel.' Given a choice, I preferred someone to understand my situation, even though she was helpless to fix it, rather than the other way around. But that's just me." **Bees. Pg 258**

Amateurs are best

That is why caring is for amateurs. There is definitely a place for professional caregivers: we need counselors, therapists, social workers and pastors who sit with the distressed and help them move ahead when tough times set in. But Jesus depends mostly on amateurs to show loving kindness in this world. The very word, amateur, means: "those who are in it for the love of it, rather than the money." The word amateur is derived from the Latin word *amare*, which means "to love". It is a beautiful thought. God needs people who do it for the love of it. It makes sense. The world will never have enough professionals. We all need care, kindness, compassion and encouragement everyday. Bring on the amateurs!

There is something revolutionary about designating God's amateurs as the primary cadre of helping folk. When combined with "just show up", the formula is a potent prescription to recruit God's people for action. Everybody is eligible. Everybody is needed. Everybody can participate in brightening this world as Jesus' "lights".

I John 4:12 makes this surprising declaration:

No one has ever seen God;
if we love one another,
God lives in us
and his love is perfected in us.
I John 4:12

This declares that God's love is made evident in this world, is expressed in this life, by us. Otherwise, God's love cannot be clearly seen. <u>What an exciting challenge and responsibility!</u>

Varieties of showing up

"Showing Up" takes many forms. Some ways are so simple: At prayer request time in our Bible Study class, a woman sitting alone in the third row began to cry as she spoke of her need. Debbie Bourne, in the row directly in front of her, quietly reached back with one hand and placed it on her knee in a reassuring manner. Crying like that is seen often. But usually others allow the weeping one to cry alone. Debbie showed up with a caring touch.

At the Memorial service I led in Stanton for Natalie, the wife of City Commissioner Harry Dotson, a large crowd gathered. I knew only the immediate family. Then I spotted two others I know well, Bill Bryant and Sue Beck. Both had visited the dying woman and her husband as pastoral care volunteers. That was their only connection, yet there they were, sitting reverently among the throng who'd come to bid a proper farewell to the woman. That these two showed up was very surprising. Their absence would never have been noticed. But they came to show they cared. Their message of compassion was extraordinarily loud and clear.

When my Dad died two years ago at age 98, most people commented adequately that "he'd lived a good life" and that "it is a blessing he's with the Lord". One card mailed to me stood out from among the many predictable pat answers, all of which were nevertheless appreciated. It said, "It hurts to lose a Father, at any age." The author of that note "showed up" with an understanding heart. The other cards were wonderful, too. The people who gave them helped me the moment the card came out of the envelope. But, mostly, their efforts to say things to make me feel better were futile. They did not have to say anything; by sending a card, they had showed up and that was enough.

I wrote an article about Care and Kindness that was published in **The Banner**, our denominational publication that is subscribed to by about 40,000. It was an upbeat article about Care and Kindness prominently placed in the periodical. I was paid, and expected nothing more. From the thousands of readers, however, I received the surprising gift of two letters thanking me for what I had written. Two showed up! I had not expected any, so what a gift those two were to me! I have no recall of what they said in their notes, but I will never forget that they wrote.

It reminds me of when Jesus healed the ten with leprosy. Later, just one bothered to look Jesus up to express his thankfulness. Only one showed up. Showing up is not a common response. Like me with my article, maybe Jesus expected none, either.

When my wife, Linda, was scheduled for surgery, notice of the operation appeared in our Sunday church bulletin, which is read by ten thousand each week. On the Sunday it was printed, some caring people spoke to me about her challenge. It was a way they could show up. All that most said was, *"I see Linda is having surgery."* Little more. It is sufficient to show thoughtfulness and concern.

90% is showing up

"Thank you so much for the message you left on my answering machine," she gushed. *"It really carried me through a difficult weekend."* It wasn't the first time I heard that kind of appreciation. Always, I am mildly stunned. Such a small contribution — such a big reaction to a recorded message!

People are thankful for acts of kindness, no matter how little. Usually there is minimal recall of the substance of the contact. The woman who so much appreciated my recorded greeting will not forget that I called but what I actually said will slip quickly away.

It is easy

It is easy to make a phone call to a hurting person. But the average man or woman neglects the kind act of making such a call. As greatly as such touches are appreciated, as elementary as the procedure of doing it is, the calls are done rarely. Too rarely. When we reach out to a struggling friend or relative, or even a neighbor or stranger, with a word, touch, card or call, we give them a shot in the arm. It works like a dose of good medicine. It is good medicine. A lot of healing flows from simple acts of Care and Kindness.

I called a friend to inquire about his well-being during his course of chemotherapy. His wife answered and said, *"Thank you for having the courage to call."* Courage?? Is that what it takes? Apparently. Why else would kind folks put off these spirit-lifting contacts? It must be fear—or lack of courage.

Needless fears

When I ask people what they fear, they always say, *"I'm afraid I will say the wrong thing."* They fear hurting the person with inane or inappropriate comments, trite reflections or bad advice. They do not realize that they cause greater harm to the struggling soul when they stay away, when they leave the person alone. It is easier to forget a poor choice of words than to forget a friend's absence.

Happily, most of the time, the hurting person overlooks inadequate words and flawed ideas that are uttered in trying to make them feel better. Brilliant remarks aren't needed. Saying "hello" is.

When you make contact with anyone recovering from, or in the middle of, a trying challenge, *"hello"* may be the main thing. After that, listening takes over as the one called on—who needs to talk—jumps at the opportunity afforded by your contact. Nothing to fear. Talk flows spontaneously from most distressed souls when they are given a chance to share how it is with them.

Make a call

If you have read this far, you may now want to turn your energy into action. Think of someone you could contact. Follow through. Set aside all reservations—fear, apprehension, nervousness, and especially all rationalizations that the call is not necessary. You will bless yourself by touching another. Pray for the courage to reach our and touch, but then make the call, even if you are frightened or nervous.

Now that you've made your call —one more thought. There is a time to break the "just show up" law. There is a time when Care and Kindness takes the opposite turn. There is a time to <u>not show up</u>.

Sometimes, "don't show up!"

After seven years of waving the banner, saying, **"90% of Helping is Just Showing Up"**, a footnote must be added. The original slogan did not intend to motivate people to make sure that they go and visit every last friend, neighbor or colleague sidelined by illness or adversity — no matter what. No, the message of the showing up rule is that you need not be a fluent speaker or an articulate encourager to be able to lift another's sagging spirits. Your presence, merely sharing a smile, a touch, or a promise of prayer, is an enormous boost most of the time. Saying wonderful sentences is not a criterion for encouragement. But you need not make a visit to all who are sidelined. There is a time to not show up at a bedside. You must <u>assess carefully if the visit is likely to be appreciated</u>.

There are occasions where the hurting person needs solitude and rest. Sometimes the wounded is already so surrounded with help or helpers that another presence is wearisome. This is most likely in an acute care hospital situation. Many patients are going through a crisis, including pain or discomfort. Some need solitude badly. Often the patient is recovering after surgery and is drained to the core. So visits to acute care facilities call for thoughtful assessment and, probably, consultation with family members of the hospitalized.

None of the above possibilities ought to be used to excuse oneself from visiting, but they should be carefully thought about. Then you might conclude that the planned visit should be postponed or cancelled.

There are also a number of folks who, at times, just plain do not want visitors. My friend, Bill Bryant, is one of those. He quips regularly, *"90% of helping is Not showing up."* Again, it is a judgment call on how much such sentiments are honored or disregarded. As a Pastor, I often disregard the little signs on the door that proclaim "No Visitors". When I do that, I certainly make it a brief stop. But those who are not Pastors need to respect the preference to be left alone. Violating such personal wishes could make the patient more ill, delay recovery, or irritate them.

It takes energy to be visited. Be brief.

Medical care and hospital treatment have changed radically in the last twenty years. Hospital stays are usually brief. Admission to a hospital implies something at a peak of intensity calling for immediate treatment. Therefore, such patients are unlikely to be having a leisurely stay. Their confinement may be only a day or two, so the need for visits may be different. In these instances, those who do show up are advised to make the stay brief. Two or three minutes may be enough —ten minutes is maximum. Remember, when you enter a room, the patient is often going to try to be an appropriate host. The work of hosting a visitor is not easy; it may be tiring at a time that the patient ought to be conserving energy.

Since most hospital stays are so short, supportive care may better be pointed toward the patient's time back home after discharge. Those are far less busy times and they may also be lonely times. There are no nurses, physicians, physical therapists, or dieticians to keep them company, and family members may have returned to their places of employment. Phone calls and personal visits to a patient's residence may be far more valued and appreciated.

Who is it for?

So, ponder first when heading for a hospital. Ask yourself, *"Am I doing this for her or for myself? Does she need this or do I?"* This is tricky business. We often are motivated by external or internal pressures that are other than what is the very best for the person. It might be an Elder's concern with just doing her duty as a church leader. It might be a neighbor's feeling that he owes this because he himself had been called upon when he was in the hospital. One can be driven by sympathy, unmodified by thoughtful consideration of the real need.

How to do it briefly

None of this should inhibit us from making a visiting call, in the sense of giving us a way out of something uncomfortable. However, if the patient doesn't clearly need our presence, either put it off until she gets home or make a short phone call to her room. If you cannot restrain yourself, be brief. Very brief! Walk in (without appearing hurried), take her hand in yours, say, *"I just want to say a prayer for you"*, close your eyes and speak a thirty second prayer for God's presence and healing. Then turn with a smile and depart with the sincere words, *"You are in our prayers."*

The patient's needs are the primary concern and caring people thoughtfully consider what is the best course of action. Most of the time, God needs our help, but sometimes God needs our help from a distance, praying.

But sometimes, longer is better

These cautions are rarely true in Assisted Living, Home Care or a Nursing Home. There, loneliness reigns! There, it is rare that we can justify "Not Showing Up". Most "seniors" need visits.

Nearly half of those living in nursing homes have no living children. More than half have no relatives at all to support them. Only one third of those living in such facilities have regular visitors. The need for mobilizing God's people is obvious and urgent.

Leaving these brothers and sisters alone in their loneliness reflects a flaw in human nature. People naturally gravitate toward rewards, and the super-elderly appear to have little to offer. They usually have little money, minimal influence, narrowed interests, reduced energy and limited futures. Even the capacity to invest in the life of their visitors is often meager or absent.

Our visits must be driven by fundamental loving kindness rather than what we will get out of this effort. We must reach out because it is right and good. Such species of kindness are morally more lofty by far than ordinary good works that directly or indirectly are driven by the rewards or satisfactions available.

Seniors have stories to tell

Not that visits to the Super-Elderly are lacking in satisfactions and benefits. All are God's beloved and every one has a story to tell. There is a wonderful gratification in caringly drawing out the details of the long life of an octogenarian. What a joy to see the light in the eyes of an older person as their memories are shared. Older folks "come back to life" when they tell their stories to an attentive listener, even if it is in bits and pieces.

Reaching out to the residents of care facilities is the new frontier, still largely unexplored. From a distance it may look frightening and uninviting. And there is difficult and daunting terrain in many places. But there is an abundance of fertile ground also available. In fact, it is a territory flowing with milk and honey, once we claim it.

More than any perspective is that truth that kindness extended to the aged is the right thing to do. Kindness directed there is a form of honoring our Mothers and Fathers, even when they are technically unrelated to us.

Jesus said to the Apostle John, from the cross, "Behold your Mother." He was entrusting his Mother Mary to John's care. This is how each of us can think of the lonely strangers we reach out to. They are God's beloved, entrusted to us.

Show up—somehow

There is little reason for compassionate people to fear reaching out to the elderly or even the most severely ill or injured. It is doubtful a caring person can legitimately justify staying away or neglecting a contact with a grieving, ill or injured acquaintance, or a senior.

The suffering, the afflicted, the struggling need care from common ordinary followers of Jesus. It is part of the medicine of recovery. And it is simple. Everyone can contribute to the healing process. It just takes showing up in some way. It means making a contact—somehow.

Yes, there is a time to modify our approach. No, there is never a time when we are not needed at all. Yes, we must adjust our timing. No, we can never act as if we are irrelevant to another's well-being. God needs our help.

> Dear children,
> let us not love with words or tongue
> but with actions and truth.
> **I John 3:18**

Discussion questions for Chapter 4 are on pages 231–234.

୬୧୬୧୬୧୬୧

Kindness Example

John L. Allen's friends had a hard time arranging care for their dog when they went on an ocean cruise. The dilemma inspired John: after the cruise, he left a note at each of the other twenty-four apartments in his complex. He offered to care for their pets, including walk the dogs, water their plants, give rides to the airport, and to help with any other need they might face when they had to be away for awhile.

Reflection: Tangible care and kindness can take expansive shapes. What a tremendous offer John presented! Those who receive such an offer come in many sizes and outlooks, so the response to John's generosity may include distrust or opportunists who take advantage of him. It is true caring and vulnerability when we expose ourselves to unexpected and even hurtful responses. This is an example of a follower of Jesus putting himself on the line with no strings attached. He just saw a need and offered to fill it.

୬୧୬୧୬୧୬୧

ঌঌঌঌঌঌঌ

Kindness Example

Dr. Jan Pfeffer sent this story about Kathy, one of her Care-persons at her Santa Margarita church. Kathy was driving her car, feeling low and discouraged, when she came up behind a pickup truck. In the back window of the truck hung a hand-drawn sketch of Jesus. The picture perked Kathy up. It lifted her mood, elevated her spirits. Then she recalled Jan's advice that we should let others know when they help us.

Catching the pickup seemed a futile effort, so she made a bargain in her mind: If he turns at the next corner, I will follow him and catch him to tell him my appreciation. To her surprise, he turned and pulled over to the curb and parked.

She offered a heartfelt gift of appreciation to a surprised and pleased young man. Both parted smiling broadly.

Reflection: You never know when your piety, pleasantness or pastime is going to bless another. So—just do it.

ঌঌঌঌঌঌঌ

ぬぬぬぬぬぬぬ

Kindness Example

Linda Jameson shares this account of loving care given to her husband, Jim.

> Jim received many acts of Kindness during his battle with cancer. The one that stood out was the dedication of two members of our class, Earl Howe and Bill Bryant.
>
> Every Friday after Jim was on Hospice, without fail, they would come over and take Jim to lunch, wheelchair and all. When Jim could no longer accompany them, they would bring lunch to the house. When he could no longer eat, they would sit and talk with him. When he could no longer talk, they would sit and talk to each other and shoo me out for some time by myself.
>
> Although Jim couldn't speak near the end, he knew they were there with him.

Reflection: Perseverance, combined with thoughtfulness, created a rare, on-going gift that endured past the point where it seemed needed.

ぬぬぬぬぬぬぬ

-5-

It's Sunday,
but Monday is Coming
(Ideas for Everyday Living and Giving)

The famous speaker, Tony Campolo, tells about a one sentence sermon preached by a Black pastor. It was a Good Friday message and the words were: **"It is Friday but Sunday is coming."** Using every possible inflection and intonation, he repeated the sentence for forty minutes, driving home the enormously potent truth that Resurrection follows Death for Jesus. Jesus' death on the cross should not be dwelled on by itself, the message said. The big news is that Jesus, after three days, arose from the grave. His life stands side by side with his death. One depends on the other. Neither should be isolated from the other.

God restores us, too

The unique sermon is intended as a powerful reminder for Jesus' followers. Not only about the incredible Easter truth that changed the world with the news that death is defeated, but it speaks to every death and death-like experience. We are supposed to know that the same God who raised Jesus from the grave will lift us up in all our death-like experiences: the losses, griefs and sorrows of everyday life. The healing presence of God will pick us up and restore us, as well.

This classic sermon needs a sequel. It should be **"It is Sunday but Monday is coming."** The point of this follow-up message is that Sunday, the day of Resurrection, is a time for regeneration and revival aimed at the week ahead. Sunday is a day of rest and refocusing. Then, on Monday morning, Jesus' people should be ready to go out with renewed energy and ideas for delivering Care and Kindness wherever they find themselves throughout the week.

Sunday is for equipping...

The Sunday morning worship service must include a commissioning, teaching and reminding that we are the "light of the world". That teaching must be aimed at mobilizing and equipping God's people to turn on and turn up our intentional and conscientious task of brightening the lives of those around us. No worship service should be complete without clear reminders and specific instruction to the congregation to display Care and Kindness everyday, everywhere they go. Likewise every person who hears the message is to be reminded that he or she has a great deal to offer others.

...for Monday

There is no Biblical text on which a sermon is built that is excused from this mandate. Whether it is Old Testament or New, the intention is to instruct, inform, and inspire God's people so they see what they are in this world for, and that they then go out and perform accordingly. Every sermon should head in the direction of leading the listeners to everyday lives that are more dedicated to making the world better—building The Kingdom.

Our place is here

The Plan of Salvation is intended to rescue us from hopeless, meaningless, dead-end futility. Salvation is intended to turn us into folks who know we are loved, valued, and cared for and that we have meaning and purpose in this life and the life to come. This tremendous information and the life-changing power it carries has responsibility wrapped up with it. The responsibility is to live conspicuously in this world, reflecting the Spirit of God that has captured us. Heaven is a bonus. Our real place is here—making the world more reflective of God, our Creator and Savior. Sunday is to prepare us for the following six days of earnest work, contributing to the improvement of life on Planet Earth.

Care and Kindness toward everybody, is one simple, needed, and possible way we can show goodness in this world and make the place better.

Gathering with other followers of Jesus on Sundays ought to be the reliable filling station to which we go to be recharged, reminded, and refocused on this spirit lifting business we are expected to be living daily. Where else can we be given such an important mandate and be motivated to put energy and thought into carrying it out? That is what Sunday church or Sunday recreation must point toward—everyday living, in a uniquely caring way toward every living person, plant and animal.

Unfinished sermons

On our vacation this summer I heard two excellent sermons in two different churches. One was about forgiveness. The other was about having a closer relationship with God. They were well done in every sense. But I thought both lacked the needed ending. Forgiveness for what? The conclusion should have been that we forgive and gain forgiveness in order to shine more brightly in this world.

The second sermon talked brilliantly about communion with God, but it stopped too soon. It needed an application to say that through a closer walk with God you will be inspired and led to greater giving to those you meet every day. Isn't that the point of closeness to God? That we are fueled to be better performers on God's wonder: Planet Earth?

If we are strongly motivated on Sunday, we will go about our business with a specific people-oriented agenda. As we visit the Supermarket, it is not just tomatoes and bread we are shopping for. We are noticing people. We are glancing at those around us and looking for opportunities to speak a word of help, encouragement, or cheer. Perhaps we merely offer a smile, or lend a helping hand. And as we pass through the checkout lane, almost always we can find a way of appreciating the cashier, or lifting her spirits by Kindness. On through the day we go, doing our work conscientiously and with integrity, but always with another agenda as well—to find ways to support, encourage, show interest toward those we meet. This is mandatory for Jesus' followers. This is our daily duty. It is not just an occasional pastime. Our minds must be set to serve others and to give them tastes of God and to make God felt in the world. That is what loving kindness is—tastes of God. Goodness is "Godness", no doubt about it.

Sunday, we pack in the ideas, inspiration, awareness, or load up on energy, refreshment and intentionality. Monday we unpack and distribute loving kindness, compassion, interest, concern and understanding.

A small but effective touch

The toll-booth official in the following anecdote had the right idea. No genius, he, but dramatically, in a small effective way, he was spreading blessings to the traveling souls who gave him their money:

> Donna D. is a daily traveler on the bridges around San Francisco. One day, the toll-taker took her coins, adding the words, *"have a wonderful day"*. Those caring words were a jolt of thoughtfulness and kindness right to the heart. Donna said it lifted her for most of the day and changed her for the better in her interactions with others.
>
> The toll-taker had dispensed a taste of God to Donna. Thoughtful words like his are part of the species we call love. Love comes from God.

I had a similar experience exiting the Budget Car Rental lot in Chicago one winter day. The final man to look at my papers handed them back with the words, "have a blessed day". I was caught off guard by such a spiritual comment, but it did bless me. His words lifted my spirits noticeably and affected me positively for several hours to come.

Eye-contact

Debbie Hutchinson told of an incident at her grocery store.

> I went to do my weekly shopping and as I walked up to the meat counter, I looked at the butcher, smiled and said, *"Hi, how are you?"* He looked at me, smiled back and replied, *"I'm fine. How are you?"* He stood there for a few moments and just stared at me. I'm sure my eyebrows were raised in wonderment as to why this man was

staring at me and then all of a sudden he said, *"Thank-you."* He said it in such an appreciative manner that it was confusing to me.

I looked at him curiously and said, *"For what?"* He said, *"Thank you for smiling at me and for asking how I am."* He walked from behind the meat counter and proceeded to say, *"Do you see that man standing over there?"* I said, *"Yes."*

He said, *"Well, he has a wedding ring on his finger but while he was placing his order with me, he was busy looking at this other lady. He never made eye contact with me as he placed his order and never said a word, other than his request for meat."*

The conversation continued and we discovered that we were both Christians and we wound up talking for about thirty minutes! I told him I worked at the Crystal Cathedral and he told me he was an Elder at his church. When people walked up to purchase meat, he would say to me, *"Wait just a minute, don't go anywhere."* Then we would continue our conversation after his customers left. I walked up to the meat counter only to order a pound of shrimp, but when I walked away from the counter I had much more than a pound of shrimp! He was very generous with the shrimp and I learned an incredible lesson. It doesn't require much to give a person a smile and to ask how the person is doing. He may have felt blessed by our encounter, but I couldn't have felt happier knowing that I made a positive difference in someone's day.

Clearly, it takes so little to make a positive difference in another's outlook, to inspire someone, to heal melancholy. It requires carrying with us the agenda of care as our mission in life, along with the more substantial occupations to which we are called.

Building hope

As Christ's Ambassadors, we are not selling something or earning something. We are trying to be responsible followers of Jesus, finding meaning in life as we endeavor to brighten the world, wherever we are. We are builders of hope as we demonstrate through supportive words, compassionate actions and consideration that there is goodness in this world.

Now let's think about getting equipped for a little more in the week ahead. "Showing Up" defines the central task (90% of it), but there is another 10% that helps the conscientious caregiver. These are some of the tools God's practitioners of Care already use and carry, but we will review them and refine them for more confident use.

To start off, let me first describe a fascinating encounter I had with a small group of my Clinical Pastoral Education students. It is an important Care and Kindness teaching.

Say Goodbye and Thank You, Please

I stirred up a hornet's nest when I pointed out to my seven CPE students that only two in the group bothered to bid me a farewell upon departure each Friday. We had met together for eight weeks, spending nearly an entire day each time in conversation and learning exercises. When adjourning, most were packing up and walking out with no acknowledgment of their host, me. Only Steven and VanderLei bade me farewell and thanked me for the day.

That bothered me. I invest heavily in these learning experiences. I dig deeply within myself and my history as a Pastor to give them everything I can. So I decided to let them know of my feelings: disappointment and irritation.

Pressing the issue further, I guessed that each of them in their careers in higher education, as students, seldom, if ever, bothered to thank their professors or lecturers after classes ended. Even though the teacher had labored for fifty minutes, giving them the best she had, often with passion and effort, they probably rushed out with total disregard for the gifts and substance that had been offered them.

Tim took vigorous exception to this bizarre suggestion that a professor should be thanked. Mandy looked stunned and thoughtful. Anette nodded as if she caught it right away. Sue supported me, and Lavonne seemed to enjoy the confrontation.

I pushed further. Had they ever left a restaurant after a dinner or lunch without presenting a gratuity to their server? Never. They agreed and appeared caught. Why so polite and appreciative in the eatery and totally oblivious of the gifts in the classroom? The question remained rhetorical, as no one had an appropriate defense, I guess.

Their behavior, however, changed radically. Now I receive handshakes, hugs, smiles and other heartwarming evidence that my presence is noticed and considered. It seems genuine—even if it is contrived. I like it. Even if it is forced, it feels better than nothing.

Break old habits

People do not change easily without threats, force, or promises of reward. This group of seven changed, I think, because they had an *"aha"* experience. There were no threats or penalties mentioned or implied. They were not bad or uncaring. They merely repeated old habits no one had ever bothered to challenge. When enlightened, they responded. My seven students are changed for life. It took effort, but the results will last forever.

Here's another way to look at this behavior, but on a much broader scale. We, who organize the Care and Kindness conference each year, are deeply gratified when we hear stories that cite actions and attitudes that have been conspicuously altered in the direction of Care and Kindness. We covet those kinds of stories because they affirm the impact of the conference. The anecdotes and other evidence shared thrill us as a confirmation that those who believe in this campaign are changed by it. So we see that the gift of this kind of feedback to conference and event organizers is the same gift my students learned to give to me.

Changes I have made

Since embarking on this project almost ten years ago, I have changed in several small ways. I frequently feel obliged to experiment, try out new behaviors, and put into practice what we are so urgently talking about. Here are some of the specific ways I am acting differently:

1. The first way I have changed is in my interaction with employees in stores, banks, gas stations and other places of business. I consistently make eye contact, smile, use their names when a name tag is present, and in parting, hand over a compliment or some words of appreciation. It is easy to do. It just requires a conscious intention, a little thought and a small effort. The results are not always obvious, but usually, clearly, a tired heart has been touched.

Almost always, a genuine smile is produced: a satisfying reward that I enjoy.

And I believe that often these simple gifts generate Hope in someone in whom Hope may have been waning.

2. The second way is small, also, but rewarding as well. It is a thoughtful agenda to greet folks more actively when walking around a mall, the neighborhood, or elsewhere.

    The results have been satisfying. For instance there is the middle-aged guy whom my wife and I often pass on our morning walks. Usually he is approaching, or is inside his rather aged automobile. When inside the car, he is grinding the starter, trying to get it running. (It never starts easily.)

    Finally one day I said, *"Good morning."* (This is harder when no previous eye contact has been offered.) He turned, gave a slight grin, and greeted us. Ever since that morning, he sees us coming and readily bids us a good day. We are like friends as a result of one greeting forced upon him.

    Another satisfying interchange happened when we passed another middle-aged man getting into his car early one morning. I said to him, *"You look sharp."* I said it because he was well groomed, with a white shirt, tie and suit coat. He smiled and told us how he had been unemployed for a long time and his unemployment compensation had expired, so he went to Hollywood and signed on to be an Extra in movies or TV. He told us he'd been kept very busy, earned a little in the process, and that it sure beat doing nothing. He seemed radiant that he could tell us about his innovative approach to unemployment.

3. A third commitment I have made is, when possible, to consistently approach speakers, performers, musicians, teachers and others after they have made their presentations. I head for the front to thank and appreciate personally the work of him or her who has just given their best effort. Most often, I am up there one-to-one with the person. All others have headed directly for the exit.

4. A fourth small idea I am carrying out, with moderate consistency, is to give at least a brief word of acknowledgment for emails sent: the humorous ones, the patriotic or spiritual kinds, so consistently received. Sometimes it is just "thanks". Whether appreciated or not, I will offer a word.

5. A steady trickle of death announcements come to my office from church members. Parents, grandparents, spouses and others reach our lists. My newest resolution is to call each who is grieving the death of a dear one, even if the primary caregiver is another pastor. The loss of a loved one deserves the utmost attention.

These are small examples of conscious efforts to connect with people a little more personally; to show interest; to show that I care; to give the gift of appreciation, or at least to notice them as human beings.

It is easy
To carry out my campaign and to practice what I preach is simple, but it does require constant thoughtfulness. It

easily slips away in the hurry and busy-ness of everyday living. But I am committed to it and I find that it is becoming habitual and almost automatic, the more I do what I should.

It takes effort

Jesus calls us "the light of the world." Shining a little more brightly takes effort and a cognitive decision to push our selves out of our comfort zones. None are life threatening moves. But most require us to leave our comfort zones for a little while, until the change becomes natural and pleasant.

The fuel for the effort required to behave differently comes from looking to Jesus. He is the energy source that can constantly replenish us when tired, forgetful or discouraged. Looking to Jesus, we can change the world, inch by inch, and find our enthusiasm restored as needed. To repeat the earlier mantra, this is what our Sunday worship is about— refueling the agents of Jesus' love.

Three major tools

There are three major pieces that are essential to the effective Care and Kindness campaign.

- The first has to do with bringing up important but sensitive subjects in conversation—"Naming the elephant". Caring like this is sometimes risky. It can feel like we are intruding, or invading another's privacy when we inquire about delicate issues. Caring people need to take those risks more often, in the interest of showing compassion and concern.

- The second is "Check your story at the door" and is really about restraining a natural human impulse which wants badly to be expressed.

- The third is Praying—and promising to pray: an essential component of true care.

I. Naming the elephant

Bill Waterson arrived at my Saturday morning class one day with serious wounds on his face. Scabbed now, they looked to be about a week old. *"What happened, Bill?"* I asked. *"I slipped on the rocks at Newport Beach,"* he said. *"I fell flat on my face."*

We groaned together for Bill a minute, then I asked, *"Bill, how many people have asked you this week what happened to your face?"* *"None,"* he answered, *"you're the first one."*

Part of me was incredulous. The other part — the part that thought to ask — wasn't so surprised. Folks have an incredible knack for leaning around elephants of all kinds.

Imagine this: A friend invites you to her house for a cup of tea. She ushers you graciously into her living room and shows you to a comfortable chair. Tea is served. Your hostess sits down on the other side of the room. Between the two of you stands a live, full-grown African Elephant. No word of explanation is offered—she merely leans to the left or to the right as she chats.

So you do the same. A pleasant but odd visit passes with no mention of the elephant. You both act as if it isn't there. You just lean around it. During the whole time, you are in fact totally preoccupied with this gray behemoth, but in the interest of courtesy, you say nothing.

Success was failure

One of our interns reported on a pastoral call that he and his wife had paid to a recently widowed church member. They met at a restaurant for dinner, and then visited at the man's house for an hour and a half.

The intern felt pleased with the whole evening. *"Did you talk about Ruth (the deceased spouse)?"* I asked. *"Oh, no,"* he replied, *"we were able to get through the whole time without referring to her."* He said it as if he had pulled off a skillful conversational coup. He was proud of the achievement.

I sat appalled. *"A bereavement call without reference to the main character?"* I asked. *"You may have had a good time, but the dominating presence in the room was Ruth, the recently deceased. Joe was thinking of her constantly and so were you. How could you not speak of her?"*

They had 'leaned around the elephant' all evening as truly as in the fictional tea party. The intern now saw success crumble to failure as I pointed out his responsibility to introduce conversation about the grieved wife.

Grieving people report that it happens all the time. Friends, neighbors and colleagues avoid what the bereaved long for: they want to talk about the one who has died. They themselves are reluctant to insert their agenda. They quickly discover the general uneasiness of people with such delicate topics. So they wait, quietly longing for a caring soul to bring up the loved one's name, so that memories may be shared. Often they wait in vain.

When in doubt, risk it

Caring encounters call for a courageous 'naming of the elephant.' Naming the elephant is talking about the obvious, even when uncomfortable. It is daring to ask, to mention, to bring up an avoided topic. The lady with the African elephant in her living room had lived with it so long she didn't think of explaining it to her guest. The widowed church member wasn't sure his guests wanted to speak of doleful things at a time of mirth. It was up to the visitor.

> Seminarian Karl trucked off to a nursing home to look in on Harry, recently transferred there from an acute care hospital. The connection was made, a conversation ensued, and prayer closed their visit.
>
> Reporting on the encounter, Karl added that Harry was missing one leg. *"Did you ask about it?"* someone queried. *"Oh, no,"* said Karl. *"I didn't think I should do that."* A note of self-satisfaction seemed present. In truth, he "blew it". Care, most of the time, falls short when the glaring concern is sidestepped. What better to focus on than the angst of the amputation, instead of acting as if it wasn't there.

There are also gray areas when the elephant is only guessed at, or is presumed to be present.

> On United Airlines Flight 125 from Chicago, I had the great fortune of garnering an exit row seat, which for my 78-inch frame is heavenly. Across from the wide exit area was a jump seat where the Flight Attendant would sit as we took off or landed. I noticed in front of the seat, before anyone sat there, a book on the floor. It looked

like a Gideon Bible I thought, which seemed puzzling. Then the take off began and the Flight Attendant came to the seat, picked up the book and strapped herself in. She immediately started looking through the book that I knew by now to be a Holy Bible. Hmmmm, I thought, this is unusual.

Why is she reading the Bible?

I pondered whether to intrude on the woman's privacy. Certainly, I thought, there is something going on in her life to cause her to be reading the Bible on the job like this. I decided to name the elephant that I guessed was behind this. So I said, *"You're reading the Bible."* She looked up and said, *"Yes, so?"*

"A little unusual," I responded. *"Oh, I don't think so,"* she replied. I let her answer sit for a minute. Then I said, *"What happened?"*

"What do you mean," she asked. *"Something happened,"* I said. *"Not really,"* she replied. *"I think something happened,"* I pressed. She said nothing. I waited, looking at her. She looked up and the tears began to flow.

"What happened," I asked gently once more. By this time she was weeping and took about five minutes to dry up her tears. Then she got up to go to work, since we had been informed that we had to return to the Gate for a mechanic. *"I'll tell you,"* she said as she went to her duties.

Providentially, we were delayed on the ground an hour and a half. So she told me the whole story.

She needed a hysterectomy and thought she might also have gall bladder trouble but had been postponing care because her father had died, her cousin had been murdered and her man-friend had dumped her. La Vonda then gave me her phone number and address, after I insisted I wanted to be encouraging and supportive to her. By this time she had learned I was a Pastor, so I assume she trusted me with this personal information. I have been true to my promise and continue in a praying and supporting role with her.

Right or wrong?

Should I have intruded, named the elephant as I did? Some whom I asked were uncomfortable that I had invaded her privacy. It was a judgment call on my part. I justified my actions on the grounds that I thought she might need support and I could possibly be of help.

Here are a couple of more examples that show the diversity of the Naming the Elephant tactic:

1) A colleague was admiring Julie Anderson's daughter; she waxed eloquently over the positive qualities of the little girl. While she was appreciating the compliments, the mother, who is a Special Education teacher, was remembering that the complimentary friend had lost a child to leukemia. Finally, Julie gently raised the tender issue. She carefully segued from her own healthy little girl to the other's heartache. The invitation was accepted and a healing conversation ensued, seasoned with tears.

2) Friends were bantering over coffee about the circumstances one couple encountered after a

dangerous house fire. The teasing centered on their temporary life in fine motels and elegant restaurants, paid for by the insurance company. The mock envy continued into the great, good fortune of replacing smoke-soaked clothing with brand new wardrobes. Laughter and hilarity prevailed. Then one of the jokesters changed her tune. *"It must have been awfully frightening,"* she offered. A brief silence followed her reflection and tears came to the eyes of the displaced couple. Suddenly a total mood change descended. The fun was over. Something very good began. Call it serious "therapy" about the horror of the devastating fire.

Well-intended behavior

Avoiding the uncomfortable, the sad, the different and the unusual is conventional behavior. Mostly it connects to not wanting to make someone or oneself uncomfortable. For example, this is the logic many follow:

> If your husband has died, I think bringing his name up is likely to trigger your tears. Therefore, I will walk around the painful and stay on the surface.

Good intentions—Faulty conclusions. True, tears are likely if we talk of the deceased loved one. But it is erroneous to think the tears are unwanted or that they signal a theme to stay away from. People want to talk of loved ones lost, even though tears flow.

Most of the time, (not always) the missing limb, the wounded face, the child who died of leukemia, the deceased spouse can be inquired about and do not need to be side-stepped. A caring person must take such risks to gain access to life's deeper levels. Skating on the surface profits little; it helps minimally. But tiptoeing into sensitive territory and inviting discussion of the 'elephant' holds the maximum potential for helpfully reaching another's hurts. The 'elephants' are topics or conditions that are clearly, but silently, in the minds of those who are present with each other. Sometimes in mentioning them, a distraction is eliminated, allowing for uncluttered interaction. Once the subject is put on the table and given appropriate recognition, other topics will be handled more effectively. This applies not only to personal one-to-one interactions but meetings involving a group of people as well.

Here is an innocuous example. I tower above most people at 6'6". When I meet new people, my height seems to distract them. Routinely I am asked, *"How tall are you, anyway?"* A quick statistic and that irrelevancy is out of the way. But until we talk about my height, that is mostly what they are thinking about.

Removing the hidden agenda

When the 'elephant' is a delicate matter, like a death in the family, the naming takes on a different color. Asking about it favors the person with true interest and concern and a care connection occurs. Even then, however, if there is other business to be done, talking of the 'elephant' has a way of temporarily releasing some pressure. Removing the hidden agenda clears the way for other important issues and other work then flows more smoothly.

Not all elephants are to be named.

It's okay to ask my height, though no one inquires of a small person, *"How little are you, anyway?"* When a death is attributed to lung cancer, little but curiosity is served by asking survivors if the victim was a smoker. Likewise, with auto crash victims and your burning question about a latched seat belt. **Don't ask!** It makes no difference now!

We were dining with a young couple and their two early-teen children. We knew the couple had been married recently and the children had come into the family with their mother. I wondered about their birth father, partly because they were such fine youngsters, polite and pleasant. The elephant in my mind was the father. But since we had only recently been introduced, I reasoned that this elephant needed to be left out of the conversation. It should not be named.

'Naming the elephant' is seldom a sure thing, but a loving tactic God's people sensitively try for, in the interest of offering loving kindness.

II. Check your story at the door

The next tactic is simple, down-to-earth courtesy. When we show up in a crisis, the one who has been hit needs to talk. It is part of the recovery process. It is also a nearly natural reflex to want to tell the whole story when something powerfully upsetting has entered one's life. Self-control on our part when we have nobly shown up includes carefully rationing our own words as we intently listen to the afflicted one talk.

This important maxim grew out of endless experiences (and we all have them all the time) of beginning to share an account of a difficult event, or telling a personal story, and then having the intended listener go off into his own long story of what happened to <u>him</u>.

> I was sitting outside the carwash waiting for my Buick to emerge. The guy next to me on the waiting bench reeked with sociability. *"How ya' doing,"* he quipped.

"Okay, except our dog just died," I said, since I was full of that sad reality. It was more than I needed to say, since this was destined to be a one-time, fifteen minute relationship. I said it in part to keep the encounter from total superficiality.

"Oh, I've been through that," responded my new best friend. And he didn't stop with this bit of non-empathy. For the next quarter hour, I listened to him about the demise of his two dogs, all the details, from top to bottom. Then his van was announced "ready" and he walked away. *"See ya',"* he said.

I was the hurting party with fresh bereavement. He was a veteran of long-past losses. I had cracked the door of lament open, but he walked in, paying no attention to my concerns. I was the patient, but I was being asked instead to become the doctor—to attend to **his** hurts.

It happens all the time. "John" shares his challenge with "Bill", but Bill responds by telling his own story. "Jane" brings up a fear, but "Betty" moves boldly onto the stage, relating her own burdens. "Sally" phones "Carole" with news, but instead, Carole seizes the opportunity to tell her own news, with little attention to what Sally had really wanted to say.

Bite your tongue

Sensitive people must bite their tongues even when they are dying to spill their own thoughts. It is the most natural thing in the world to jump over to your own memories when those of someone else trigger a recall of something similar. Stories evoke stories. But caring people diligently refrain from stealing another's spotlight. They know that if "Bob" brings up either a sorrow or a joy, Bob is asking to be heard—not to have the tables turned so that he has to listen while you share.

I visited "Agnes" in Memorial Hospital after her major surgery. She'd had an operation to remove a brain tumor. As I sat beside her bed, one throbbing thought was clamoring in my head—my mother's brain tumor surgery, decades earlier. I wanted badly to tell Agnes my story. Here was a point of identification to pull us together. "See, I understand this," my telling would prove.

Better judgment, however, kept my tongue still. This was Agnes' dilemma for me to reach out toward—not a time for her to minister to me, as inevitably would happen. (Even the mention of my mother's illness could not be considered. Agnes would certainly want to know the outcome. Since my mother died of her malignant tumor, this was definitely not a tale to tell a person fresh from the operating room.)

Resist mightily the strong temptation to discontinue tuning in to another's story in order to tell your own. As powerful as your similar incident might be, if another person has handed you his or her joy or sorrow, stay with it. Yours can wait.

A sentence to avoid

One other caveat: Even if you have traveled the identical road, try to avoid the words, "I understand how you feel." No one, for sure, really knows how another feels. To say, *"I understand"* irritates more than it helps. Similar circumstances do not mean equal responses. Everybody is different. Seek to understand the other, but resist claiming that you do. Instead, it is much more helpful to show empathy for the person's pain (or joy) by saying something like, *"You must really be hurting."*

After "showing up" or being there for friends who want to talk, or open a tender subject, give them the spotlight. Use all your energy to pay attention to their joys or concerns. Save your own story for another day. "Check it at the door", so it stays safely on the sidelines. This self-discipline is one of the surest signs of a mature caregiver.

There is a time to tell your story

Now it's time to modify the "Check Your Story at the Door" law. Common sense tells us there is a time when my story will be helpful to someone going through something tough. Yes, there is a time to tell your story.

One obvious time when we want to tell our own, and it feels appropriate, is when we have been through something very difficult that is similar to that of the person to whom you are listening. To refrain from sharing your own experience may become a major turn-off if, later, he learns that you have gone through the same thing, but said nothing about it. It can feel fraudulent. Or certainly odd and puzzling.

A breast cancer survivor increases her credibility as a caring friend greatly when she briefly lets it be known, to a newly diagnosed patient, that she has been through it herself. Likewise, with a man who has had, for example, prostate surgery. Other examples could be added. They help a struggler gain hope as he sees a survivor living fully after the same challenge. Not only that: by identifying yourself as one who has gone through something similar, you are now a resource the other can reach out to for information, advice and guidance. This can be very much appreciated.

Brevity is essential

The keys to sharing one's own story are brevity and helpfulness.

1) Your account must be a brief side trip that increases your credibility as a caring helper. Now he knows that you are personally familiar with this kind of challenge.

2) Secondly, it should draw from your own experience the information and feelings potentially useful to the other.

Like this: If visiting someone grieving the death of a child: *"We went through the death of our son and it was devastating. This must be for you just terribly difficult."* This statement briefly refers to one's own experience while it draws out a description of how awful it was as a way of conveying compassionate understanding. After saying that much, the presently grieving parent is listened to again. That grieving parent may then, or later, inquire about how the visiting parent coped with such a terrible loss or ask for other needed information.

Here is an example shared by Pastor Don from a conversation he had with a Jiffy Lube manager, whom he knew slightly, and whose brother had just died:

Jiffy Lube: *"I sure hope this year turns out better. I have had some financial problems. I forgot to cash my check last week, so the bank is upset. I just forgot, with my brother's death and all"*

Pastor Don: *"I know what you mean. When my Dad died in April, I forgot a lot of things,* *including what hours I was working at the hospital one day. It's part of grieving, I guess."*

Quickly he communicated empathy and let the other know his own pain. Then he paused so Jiffy Lube could resume.

Keeping it succinct is not always easy. If we are recalling a trauma of our own, plenty of emotion is still there. Rarely, if ever, is it totally erased from our hearts. When we open the door to say a little, it is the most natural thing to start telling the whole story. Old hurts always need more therapy. Talk helps. But when reaching out to others in the thick of their tough time, we must vigilantly guard their opportunity to talk after we briefly tell our own experience.

Instead of totally "checking your story at the door", carry it in with you, and dole it out thoughtfully when you think it may be helpful.

III. Care and the power of prayer

The third element in my trio of major pieces essential to effective Care and Kindness is prayer, an indispensable part of the way caring people touch those in distress. Prayer is about people's connection to God. When we pray or promise prayer, we remind people of that connection and we use it for their well-being. We personally go to God and ask for help for the hurting person.

When I teach prayer to our New Hope Telephone Counselors, some of them have never prayed out loud for another person in their entire life. They are terrified about praying. I reassure them by saying, *"If you can order a Hamburger at the drive-through at McDonalds, you can ask God for what your hurting caller needs."* That is how simple and easy prayer really is.

Care without prayer is inadequate to most followers of Jesus. It is almost like the role of antibiotics in infectious diseases; its use is automatically included. So to write about Care and Kindness without stressing prayer would be an unfortunate oversight.

Some have talked of prayer as "Healing at a Distance". With this in mind, I would like to share an account written by my wife, Linda, about part of her breast cancer surgery challenge and the way prayer supported her:

My Journey Through Breast Cancer

Have you ever wondered how your Christian faith would help you in times of crisis? I often did. The answer came through the strong, unwanted challenge of breast cancer in 1996.

My first reaction to the diagnosis was shock and disbelief because I felt so healthy, and I had religiously gone through the mammogram process. But the doctor confirmed what only the ultra sound revealed, that each breast had malignant tumors. Furthermore, because of their types, a double mastectomy was the highly recommended solution. It was confirmed by other physicians and my unwelcome journey was underway.

*Prayer chains at the Crystal Cathedral and all over the country sent word they were praying for me. **I felt these prayers**. My husband said he felt the prayers also. How did we FEEL them? They created a sense of calmness that this was all in the Lord's Hands. Although I was nervous and uncertain about the future I knew that my life was a gift of God and when it ended He* *would take me home. I have always believed this. It was a great comfort, even though I desperately prayed this was not to be the time.*

An unexpected angel

Finally the day for surgery arrived. It was Good Friday! Though I was alone in surgery my husband, family, and about 20 church staff, members and friends gathered in the Hospital Lobby to wait and pray for me. What a blessing! Their presence lifted and carried me.

*When I came to, groggily, after surgery, in the Recovery Room, I was in excruciating pain. I called, as best I could, to the nurse on duty and begged for medication. But she was overly busy and brusquely replied, "No pain medication yet!" As I lay there with ripping agony across my chest, an uplifting thought floated through my mind. Simply this: "**Positive Prayers and Praise.**" As that unusual phrase filtered through my consciousness, to my amazement, my pain ceased. About every five minutes, in that first difficult hour of recovery the pain re-occurred and each time my uniquely worded thought, "**Positive Prayers and Praise**" flowed back in to totally erase the pain. I believe this was a MIRACLE - God's way of reassuring and comforting me. I also interpret it as a mysterious benefit of the prayers underway at the moment, and many years of hearing and trusting Christian messages.*

Finally, I was taken to my room. The first words I heard there were warm and kind. I instinctively reached out to touch this new friend, a staff nurse. To my surprise she said she knew me— she was from our church, the Crystal Cathedral. It seemed impossible. Another miracle? She cared for me like an Angel — kind, comforting, and loving. During my three day stay she always looked out for me and made sure I had the best nurse available when she wasn't on duty. She was a gift from God, named Kathy Crane.

Flowers, cards, gifts flowed in, all expressing their love and prayers for recovery. How they helped! Each added something to lift my spirits. I was overwhelmed with a feeling of love and peace. Arvella Schuller wrote, "Linda, you have given to others so much. Now it is payback time. People will want to help. Let them and enjoy it!" How true and helpful were her words.

When I went home my family and friends were there for me again. Two of my sisters, Martha and Diana, came to help so my husband could go back to work. Believe it or not I returned to the classroom in five weeks, teaching kindergarten full-time. How blessed I was! Loving kindness had picked me up in a big hurry.

Six weeks after surgery I started chemotherapy. When chemo was finished, breast reconstruction began.

As I look back on that year and half period, I find that neither my husband nor I remember it as a nightmare or terrible ordeal. Of course, we wouldn't choose to go through it again, but during it all we continued to enjoy our lives.

Constant prayers, *encouragement, cards, and gifts of flowers and food from friends bolstered our feelings of optimism and hopefulness.*

Key points that I learned through this experience:

1. Great results can be achieved with God through prayer.

2. The great army of Christians throughout the world help in many ways to be supportive.

3. Talented medical people! Incredible nurses and staff are God's special servants.

4. My extremely loving and supportive husband believing "You can do it!"

One more thing. I received tons of Get Well cards. I appreciated every one of them. They helped me. Of the hundreds I read, all but two said something like "You are in our prayers" or "We are praying for you." Two said "We are thinking of you" or "You are in our thoughts." I valued those also, but in comparison to being thought about, the active care of being prayed for felt so much more helpful. **Linda Kok**

Linda felt the prayers relieve her pain as the unusual words "Positive Prayer and Praise" flowed into her consciousness, but she also relished and felt lifted by her awareness of caring prayer winging its way towards her from scores of sources. Just knowing that prayers were circling her from near and far strengthened her.

My experience

My own experience with prayer is anecdotal, as well. In my case, it was a very minor affliction.

> One week in winter, beginning on Monday, I was felled by a terrible cold and influenza-like symptoms. Bed was the only place I felt like being those days.

> Surprisingly, mid-morning on Wednesday, I felt a surge of renewed energy, my fever was gone and my distress was lessened. This kept progressing until I was in full recovery by Friday and able to go back to work.

> A number of days later a colleague casually remarked that they had prayed for me at the Staff devotions a couple of weeks previously. *"Really?"* I remarked. *"When was that?"* As the day and time was pinpointed, I realized it was at the very moment that I had felt that sense of renewed health in a surprising way. I retain the conviction that it was their prayers that caught me just right and refreshed my health that week.

One other powerful experience bolstered my confidence in the power of prayer. It happened over thirty years ago when I was a hospital chaplain.

> A young seminarian chaplain intern named John De Vries and his wife Ellie were being blessed with the birth of their first baby when something went wrong. John called me and informed us that the baby could not live because of a "Hyaline Membrane" condition that was beyond repair or

correction. It was a dreadful outlook and terribly sad.

I remember turning that evening, in the direction of the hospital, and breathing an especially intense prayer that the baby would live. Hundreds of others were praying also, of course.

At six the next morning the telephone rang. It was John. Something had happened! The baby was doing well and it looked like he would live after all. That baby is over thirty years old now, in 2004, and is very healthy.

To this day, I feel that was a recovery wrought by the power of prayer.

Research on prayer

Something else has bolstered my confidence in prayer in the last ten or fifteen years. I read about a research project in a San Francisco Hospital Cardiac Care Unit, where the plan included dividing the patients in two equal groups—similar ages, sex, symptoms and diagnosis. Then, without informing either group A or B, group A was prayed for intensely by groups of different faiths from all over the USA. Group B received conventional spiritual treatment.

The results showed that the specially prayed for group did significantly better than the other group. They used less pain medicine, had fewer infections, were discharged earlier and had less death. Prayer apparently had made a measurable difference for Group A.

I have read that similarly constructed experiments have produced the same results, which is a necessity before trusting any research.

Stories nourish our souls

The final variable I want to mention is the constant trickle of positive reports from a church group of about 75 people at The Crystal Cathedral who meet together each week for Bible study and fellowship. The members of the class, called The Becomers, routinely talk about their prayer needs to each other and as time passes, tell about the favorable outcomes they attribute to prayer. Their care for each other in the group is inspiring and strengthening to all the members.

Anecdotal evidence has fed the Christian church since its onset. To this day followers of Jesus find their spirits encouraged and their faith nourished by the simple stories of good things happening in the praying community.

Jesus taught us to pray

Nevertheless, the primary reason most people pray is because Jesus taught us to pray. It is just part and parcel of what caring souls do on behalf of others. We pray because it is part of our identity as His followers. Letting someone know we are praying for him is a message of care and concern highly valued by almost everyone. Just being informed that you are being prayed for and remembered in prayer is a spirit lifting experience in itself. I have told nearly complete strangers, after hearing their struggle, that I will pray for them without even knowing if they are believers in prayer or believers in anything. Nearly always the response is wide-eyed appreciation. They receive the promise as a caring act of an especially heavy and personal nature.

The shape of prayer

I think of prayer in a triangular shape. On the one hand, my prayer goes up to God and God sends His sustaining and loving presence to the one being prayed for. In addition, I hold the prayed for in my heart and mind and consciously send love, concern and compassion horizontally his or her way. I firmly believe that we are God's transmitters when we pray that way. We are literally sending God's energy and love as we close our eyes, concentrate lovingly, and send our concern and love in the direction of the one cared for at the moment.

If you say it, do it!

It is easy to say, *"I'll be praying for you."* Too easy, sometimes. One of the alerts I remember from my early pastoral training is about promising to pray for people. We were warned not to let those words too easily flow from our lips. To this day, that advice affects me. I rarely say *"I'll be praying for you"* unless I am determined to do so. It is an important issue. If the promise is going to have strengthening power in itself, it must come from a sincere and committed heart that will follow through. Otherwise, the words are destined to become a mere salutation or a farewell, meaning little.

Being prayed for is an enormous gift. Those who pray conscientiously put time into their supplications. They exert energy. They think about the situation and the need. Their hearts are heavy with concern and love. To offer this is a wonderful gift. To be offered prayer should be thoughtfully appreciated. A warm, moving and grateful response is an appropriate way to say thank you.

Marching orders and basic equipment

Followers of Jesus have a very specific responsibility seven days a week. In every aspect of our lives, we are expected to be helping to answer Jesus' prayer, "Our Father in Heaven...Thy will be done on earth as it is in heaven." Our work is a contribution to making this world a better place. Our Sunday experience and all our worship, study, and devotions must aim at contributing to that goal.

Beyond our work, and wrapped up with it, are our relationships. Every shade of relationship seasons our lives. Some are momentary, impersonal, as in emails and sometimes phone calls. Others are face to face with strangers and casual acquaintances at stores and businesses. There are family and other dear ones, like friends and colleagues. Every shade of intimacy needs our conscientious concern. In every instance, thoughtful behavior that shows Care and Kindness is called for.

Four tools, actually

To these three tools, we join the primary need to "show up". So we have these <u>four</u> strategic tools that will change a person's life—the serious ambassador of goodwill needs each of them. They will turn the average pleasant person into an effective helper of others.

- **Showing up,** coming to the person with concern in your heart.

- **Doling out your experiences cautiously and tentatively,** the courtesy of respecting another's need to talk.

- The risky venture we call **Naming the elephant** that can open doors into the depths of another's heart in surprising ways.

- **Prayer,** that indispensable ingredient that changes things so positively by connecting to God on behalf of someone else.

Internalize these strategies; soak in them; incorporate them into your daily life. They will revolutionize your relationships. You will have the equipment to turn every conversation into a deep encounter, if you wish. So we have our marching orders and a few ways to make our behavior truly helpful. Start today to practice what we preach.

> ...live such good lives among the pagans that,
> though they accuse you of doing wrong,
> they may see your good deeds
> and glorify God...
> **I Peter 2:11–17**

Discussion questions for Chapter 5 are on pages 234–238.

ഏഏഏഏഏഏ

Kindness Example

Ken Morrow and his foursome were teeing off at the last hole, nearing the end of their early morning round of play. Right next to them a new group was teeing up on the 10th tee.

"Do you have an extra scorecard?" one called over. No one did. *"Thanks, anyway,"* they responded. Since they were walking the course and it was a long way back to the clubhouse, it looked like they were planning to manage their round without a card.

Ken, however, seized the initiative. He jumped into his golf cart, sped back to the clubhouse and promptly returned with a fresh card for the four strangers.

Reflection—So obvious, so easy. But so easy to miss the chance, too. Ken noticed, thought, and acted.

ഏഏഏഏഏഏ

જ્જ્જ્જ્જ્જ

Kindness Example

Charlie Brown to Lucy: *"Do pretty girls know they are pretty?"*

Lucy to Charlie Brown: *"Only if somebody tells them."*

Charlie Brown: Looks stunned.

Lucy: *"Well?"*

Charlie Brown: Looks away befuddled, apparently unable to tell her straight on.

Reflection: No one is so pretty, handsome, or successful that they do not need to be given compliments.

જ્જ્જ્જ્જ્જ

Kindness Example

Last year here on our Morrison School campus, I was dashing in the rain and an unfamiliar woman handed me her umbrella! Yes, it happened! I was so struck by this simple act of kindness!

Before she could get away, I asked her for her name. It was Angela. She had the right name! She was living out her name as I met her...<u>angel</u>! I told her I'd take her umbrella to the office and she could get it later. When I did take it in to the secretary, she knew who Angela was and set it aside for her.

Aaaah. It put a smile on my face for the rest of the day.

Reflection: Sharon Williams sent in this vignette from Taiwan, where she is tutoring the child of a missionary couple. Here is her thought about the incident: *"On the whole, our world is not getting better at kindness. But let's not be deterred! When people are nice, as this stranger, it surprises me."*

Another simple act of kindness with day-long good effects.

-6-

Allow, Accept, Affirm, and Appreciate My Feelings

There is a well-intentioned urge among human beings to deny others their pain. If I sprain my ankle, someone will quickly advise me to *"be happy it isn't broken."* I have seldom found that to be an effective pain killer. It still hurts!

Don't deny me my pain

At the very foundation of the concept of caring, there lies a principle that feels counter-intuitive, or at least counter to most of our past experiences. That principle is this: allow people to feel their pain. Don't deny them this necessary step in healing. Resist trying to play it down or belittle it. Forgo reflections that compare it to someone or something worse like "think of all those in Africa with A.I.D.S." At the least, do not think it is your duty to take their pain away. Your presence and interest is an ample anesthetic.

The message in this kind of help asks us to compare a lesser injury to a greater one—that you should not feel bad. The message is also an attempt to make the stricken one feel better. I do not think this method of helping works very well. The whimpering victim of a broken fingernail already knows this is not a life-threatening injury, but she still needs to vent her frustration, so let her do it! The limper with the bad ankle knows that he will heal soon, but he is nevertheless hurting now, so let him lament. Don't be in too much of a hurry to stifle or distract such people. *(Just because I have stopped crying doesn't mean my discomfort has ended. It doesn't mean that your muffling me has helped. I probably stopped mostly because you wanted me to stop.)*

Your tears upset me

It is plausible that our earnest attempts to help another feel better are really based on our own discomfort with upset feelings. In other words, if I can get you to act and talk more cheerfully, I will also feel more comfortable and less upset. Many of our seemingly benevolent words may simply be attempts to help ourselves by calming the storms and drying the tears which bother us.

It often is far more appreciated when a caring friend says, *"I'll bet that hurts terribly,"* than if she says, *"It could be so much worse."* The chance that a pain will actually lessen seems more likely when someone recognizes it and acknowledges it with understanding words than if they try to play it down.

This means our caring endeavors are most likely to be effective when we do exactly the opposite of what we think we should do. Instead of trying to make the pain go away—which never works—we should name it as harshly as it deserves. That might, in fact, prove more healing.

Call it something else

Here's a novel way to remove problems: According to legend, Florida got rid of all its cockroaches—there are no more cockroaches in Florida, not one. The extermination process was easy and total: they simply re-named the cockroach. Now it's a Banana Beetle. Problem solved!

My dad claimed he had never had a headache. I was puzzled at this, because I recall his complaints about sinus pain (which, in my opinion, is a headache). *"Oh, yes,"* he admitted, *"I did have sinus pain, but never a headache."* Okaaay…you eliminate headaches by calling them something else.

Many people act as if they can create an atmosphere of healing by renaming or reframing the "bad stuff". This is only slightly different from the "think of all the people in Africa with AIDS" idea.

Here's how it happens: A young man, Bert, arrives at church on Sunday. He joins his friends over a cup of coffee after the service. *"I rolled my car last night on Highway 39. Hit black ice and just lost control. Totaled it, I'm sure. And I had less than 10,000 miles on it."* To this grim announcement, Tom responds, *"But you're not hurt!"*

Observation #1: The truth of Tom's statement cannot be denied; probably part of Bert is breathing the same prayer. But the effect of Tom's words is this: "you may have destroyed your car, but as long as you are walking around talking about it—you do not have a problem." Tom refuses to recognize that there is indeed cause for concern, dismay, even melancholy—because no life was lost or bodily injuries sustained.

Observation #2: Bert is feeling awful about his wrecked SUV. He loved his new vehicle. Plus, he drives to work every day. He needs transportation. The quick diagnosis that calls him to be thankful (because he sustained no injuries) confuses him. *"Yeah, you're right,"* he softly says to Tom, and the group of men slide into talk of other things, as if all that matters is Bert's intact body. Bert needs to talk about his experience in order to move on emotionally. He has been thwarted in this by Tom's glib diagnosis that Bert has no problem.

Another sad but true story:

> Maria, an elementary school teacher, learned she had a lump in her breast. Frightened, she called another teacher she knew to be an active church member. Maria poured out her plight to Karena, but when Maria paused, Karena said, *"But you know you are 'saved', Maria."* This pronouncement from Karena translated to, *"You don't have a problem."*

But Maria did have a problem. The prospect of surgery, chemotherapy, radiation, medical costs, missing work—all these things stared her in the face. She had a life-threatening fight on her hands. Being "saved" did not fix all that. Thoughts of next-life serenity hardly helped her with the challenges of the here and now. So, sadly, Maria learned during this phone call that she could not share openly with Karena. Karena implied that Maria's salvation was all that really mattered, not the life challenge ahead of her. "No problem, you are saved," said Karena.

There's nothing new about telling people they do not have a problem, even when they clearly do. In the Old Testament we read:

> They have treated the wound
> of my people carelessly,
> saying "Peace, peace,"
> when there is no peace.
> **Jeremiah 8:11 NIV**

This is paraphrased in The Living Bible even more pointedly:

> They give useless medicine
> for my people's grievous wounds
> for they assure them all is well
> when that isn't so at all!
> **Jeremiah 8:11 TLB**

Shouldn't we look on the bright side?

Why should we allow the person to feel the pain of his problem? Why not put a "spin" on it so the blunt pain of the blow is softened? It seems kind and merciful to show a hurting soul a bright side, or a positive perspective, on a seemingly negative circumstance. If a comment lifts a guy's spirits, why not say it?

The answer to this seemingly well-intentioned attitude is that just because you walked away from your totally wrecked car does not mean you have no problem. Looking on the bright side only temporarily and partially distracts you from the true challenge of a destroyed vehicle. Moving to the bright side happens most naturally when first the tears are shed, the hurt feelings are expressed, and a listening ear pays attention to the dismay and adds an understanding comment. When the fog of fright and grief lifts in the proper time, the sun will shine again.

There is a shortage of the kinds of people who can sidestep the opportunity to offer cheer, and instead reflect out loud the reality of the loss. It is a rare star who creates an atmosphere of healing by naming the "bad stuff", accepting the feelings, and hearing the story of what happened. That is what Care and Kindness looks like, punctuated by an understanding sentence or two.

The real helper sees to it that the physical needs are taken care of and then invites the hurt ones to feel their pain: to talk, lament, weep, and groan if they wish. When tears flow, things aren't getting worse; there is actually healing under way. People who understand this are friends to be treasured.

Let me repeat it again: <u>When tears flow, things aren't getting worse: there is actually healing under way when we allow and encourage the natural expression of hurt.</u>

It feels soooo good to have another human being put the truth into words, such as, *"that's really tough—to lose a valued car and nearly get smashed yourself."* or to say to Maria, *"I'm so sorry to hear that. You must be frightened."*

Our God, according to Scripture, hears our cries and is touched. Compassion defines God. It must be prominent with us, too.

There is little reason for us to act differently. Let us hear people's cries. Resist deflecting them, comparing them, calling them something else, or evaluating their validity. Just walk with them, sit with them, be with them. God will do the healing. We can leave it to God, but we must do our part.

Don't take my sadness from me

Most of us resist when people try to take our pain from us. I was aware of this when my Dad died recently at age 98. His death made me sad. But mostly, when mentioning his death and admitting my sadness, I'd hear, *"Well think of what a good long life he led,"* –or– *"Be thankful you had him so many years."*

I know he had a surprisingly good long life. I am thankful for his presence for so many years. But these realities do not make me less sad. Besides, I want to feel sad. Feeling sad is the right way to feel and I do not want to have my sadness prematurely taken from me. It will diminish as time passes. For now, I choose the sadness and resist attempts to dilute or erase it.

Since this is so important for authentic Care and Kindness, I turn now to a scriptural example, where we are shown the proper attitude in the face of another's heartache. Notice how it contrasts with our almost natural tendency to try to take folk's pain from them by one technique or another.

Weep with those who weep

Nearly 2000 years ago, The Apostle Paul told his readers how to respond to the hurting ones around them, though his timeless advice is not widely accepted in the current Christian community. Paul said "Weep with those who weep." In today's society, we are not strong adherents to this guidance. We are not comfortable with Paul's advice of mixing our tears with another's. It doesn't seem like legitimate helpfulness. We want to help stop their tears.

A childhood friend I hadn't seen in fifty years greeted me during the halftime of a high school football game. Among the reminiscences, he brought up some tender memories of my mother, who died at a young age. Tears pooled in my eyes as he elaborated, but I listened hungrily. Then he noticed my tears.

"I'm sorry," he said. He appeared to apologize for the sharing that touched me and triggered a little salty water. He rather hastily concluded the conversation and departed. I think he was disarmed by my tears, meager as they were. His moving on seemed partly to be embarrassment about my emotion and possibly also over his own feelings welling up. I stood mildly unsettled by his retreat. I wanted him to stay

and tell me more and encourage the tears—not shut them off.

Tears. What do we do with them?

My old friend, if I interpret his behavior accurately, totally miscalculated my condition. I was loving the memories he was sharing. I valued the tender feelings evoked. I loved the tears welling up in my eyes. No apology was needed. The interchange was wonderful. My tears meant "good stuff", not injury. He had given me a gift. The gift would have been even more precious had he stayed with me face to face, with his own lachrymal glands pumping.

Often people, who come to my office, sit down, try to talk, and then struggle in their fight to hold back tears. They say, *"Oh, I was so determined not to cry. I am so sorry."* My response usually goes something like this: *"It's okay. Tears are good. Let them flow. Tears are a gift of God. Take your time. Cry. I love tears."*

I love tears because they are real. When she is crying, I know she is honestly hurting. Words are not always as honest. Words conceal more often than they reveal. Tears are honest.

Never say, "Don't cry!"

We say it instinctively to little ones. We repeat it to spouses and friends when they weep. We shout it silently to ourselves in every troublesome crisis. "Don't cry!" We warn; we suggest; we plead. Maybe, most of all, we are disturbed by our own uneasiness. We are thinking, "If you cry, I am going to start feeling mushy, crummy and out of control. I hate to feel that way. So please don't cry. I can't handle it."

I can think of no time, except maybe when driving a car, where crying is inappropriate. It is too dangerous when driving a car. But other than for that reason, the "don't cry" exhortation ought to be blotted out, erased, eliminated. The words serve no good purpose. No one should ever tell another, *"Don't cry!"*

Remember, St. Paul said, "weep with those who weep." But instead, our own actions say, *"Fix their problem so they quit crying."* –or– *"Quote Scripture to those who cry."* –or– *"Tell them to give their aches to God instead of crying about it."* –or– *"Give advice to those who cry."* But weep with them? **Uh-uh**. **No**. Rarely is wound healing done St. Paul's way—by sitting in the dust, crying with the broken hearted, or with a caring embrace, mingling our tears with hers.

Tears heal

St. Paul knew that wounds heal from the inside and not by covering them up. The Band-Aids of advice, quotes, and verses accomplish little more than drying up the tears. Stopping them is damming the healing process. Modern chemical analysis reveals that tears carry specific toxic substances from the body. Crying is healing. The balm of being understood and accepted, tears and all, reaches deep. Shared tears warm the heart and aid recovery. The helping person needs to allow herself to feel the watery weakness of the wounded one in order to really enhance healing.

Other ways to weep

Literally crying with another is only one application of Paul's guidance. A second use of the teaching may be equally useful. The principle really is this: get inside the other's feelings as much as possible. Feel what she feels or try to realize what she feels. Avoid standing apart. Show that you area trying to understand her distress. To put it another way, do not move quickly to try to fix another's problem. Hold back your remedies. Stifle words of blame and questions about causes.

The following is an example to illustrate the teaching:

> Helen arrived at her place of work forty-five minutes late after her noon lunch hour. She walked in, surprisingly calm and collected—not looking frustrated—and explained, *"I locked my keys in the car at the restaurant and it took a half hour for my husband to come with another set."*
>
> Immediately one of her colleagues replied, *"What you need to do is get one of those little magnetic boxes and hide a second key under your bumper."*

An obviously necessary idea Helen can use, but right now there is no connecting with her feelings at all. No groans, no words of understanding or empathy for the lady's distress. No co-weeping here—just a completely obvious piece of advice she didn't need at this moment. Simple, minor, fixable dilemmas, like the key locked in the car, are helped very easily. The friend could just say, *"That's a bummer."* Or *"oooh, shucks."* Or *"You sure didn't need that, did you?"* Or *"That's frustrating, isn't it?"*

Each of these brief retorts makes it clear that the feelings of being upset are heard, felt and accepted. No advice. No criticism. No trivializing. No humorous belittling. No requests for information. No irrelevant questions trying to fix the blame. Just groans. (a form of "weeping with") put into words, that clearly fit the woman's frustration.

Guess at the feelings

The upset woman did not say she was frustrated or vexed. Maybe her tone of voice communicated her lousy feelings. But maybe not. She may have made a simple declarative sentence with no emotion. The good listener, putting himself into the situation, can guess her feelings. He speaks from what he knows he would feel, or has felt, in mistakes like hers. He draws from his own inner history and puts into words a response that corresponds with her feelings — even though she has declared none. And she then, no doubt, will feel understood and accepted in her exasperation. Knowing you are heard makes bitter pills go down easier.

Use the "third ear"

I like to teach people to listen with their "third ear." This means hearing the feelings, even when they are not clearly stated or mentioned. "I locked my keys in the car," says nothing of how she felt about it. The "third ear" hears frustration and then puts words to that feeling. Even a groan would communicate understanding here. "Our dog died," includes no overt cry of distress, and yet everyone can guess about the sadness there and emit an appropriate, *"Oooh, that's sad."*

A groan helps

A groan can be a valid form of weeping with another person. So can a simple heartfelt "bummer". A sentence that articulates the upset or irritation of another also fits the "weeping" exhortation. *"It sounds like you are really at the end of your rope,"* is a well-spoken summary of someone's exasperation or despair. It feels like solid, thoughtful compassion. That is what the "weeping with" idea is about.

Say what you guess they are feeling

When something dreadful happens to another, we may have a pretty good idea they are feeling sad, afraid or frustrated. Then we need to find a way to communicate our understanding that they are feeling sadness, fear, or frustration. No one can automatically know that we understand or are feeling badly with them. We must send a message, disclosing we are feeling for them. We may be agonizing inside, but others cannot see it.

The words must be spoken

In the caring process, a statement makes it clear. Saying something like, *"You're really feeling frustrated"*, shows we realize their feelings and do not judge them for their frustration.

Reality, then, is this: the most helpful response to another's crying is to let our own instinctive tears and empathy gush—to feel or realize what another is feeling and to let them know it.

> A middle-aged woman walked into a grief recovery group. She shared that her reason for being there was the death of her son in a motorcycle accident. Not many minutes had passed when another woman asked, *"Was he wearing a helmet?"*

She asked the question everyone was wondering. A pressure inside us seems to clamor to know if neglect of a helmet contributed to the fatal injury, but asking about the helmet is a long way from empathy. Asking a factual question is a major distance from weeping with, groaning with, or speaking words of understanding. The curiosity must be stifled because asking gets at blaming; it sidesteps a mother's despair, and at this point it makes no difference if he was or was not wearing a helmet.

In times of emotional distress little is gained by soliciting information about causes or who was to blame. Help comes from a clear, caring message, whether tears, groans, a touch, a hug or just showing up.

A good example of "being with"

One of the most beloved of all Bible passages is Psalm 23. One reason for the universal love for this Psalm is the picture of The Shepherd being with the sheep. "With" is the key word. The Shepherd walks with, accompanies, cares for us. There is no word of fixing, solving or advising.

Nevertheless, "He restores my soul." Restoring stands out. It sounds like the process of healing, emanating from caring companionship, loving attention, empathy and understanding. "Even though I walk through the valley of the shadow of death...you are with me." Walking with others is a metaphor borrowed from the 23rd Psalm for the way that helping and healing happens.

St. Paul has a pertinent line that applies here:

> Your attitude should be the same
> as that of Christ Jesus
> [the great Shepherd of the Sheep]
> **Philippians 2:5**

May the spirit of Psalm 23 lead us in responding to the hurts of others. It is the essence of supportive companionship in difficult times. When we live like that with others, we, too, will help to restore their souls, and it happens mostly by being with them.

Since this subject is vitally important, I would like to specifically talk more about what it takes to bring comfort to another person when they are knocked down by one of the harsh blows of life.

What words comfort a sorrowing soul?

Besides "being with", what can help the devastated feel a little better when their dearest friend is taken away, or when a life-long job is lost? Is there an action, a word, an answer that lessens the pain? Is there anything that can make a positive difference?

Everybody wants to help when tragedy strikes—to comfort, to lift, to cheer. Whatever is done or said is intended and believed to make the afflicted feel better. So the words, attitudes or behaviors used on behalf of one who is heartbroken are delivered, thinking they are beneficial in healing the heartache.

Good words that do not help

Let us look at a specific situation and analyze the effects of well-intended sentences delivered to young parents suffering from the accidental death of their healthy six-year-old.

First, here is a supposedly comforting sentence that is commonly given:

"Try to remember she is with the Lord." For the grieving parent, of course, there is comfort in this important truth. It is a powerfully vital hope, but saying this does little to lessen the terrible pain of their child's death. Certainly their outlook is affected by Easter hope, but there is virtually no softening of their devastating loss by reminders of the child's ongoing life in Jesus' presence.

As crucial as this truth may be, when anyone attempts to comfort by using this spiritual concept, the grief-stricken will feel it to be spoken by someone who doesn't understand. Uttering this key theological doctrine to parents who are "broken and bleeding" only silences them from speaking of their anguish until a more understanding friend comes along. Such theological truths, because they lack heartfelt understanding, distance the speaker from the victim. Such "comforts" leave them feeling more alone and maybe even resentful.

These words do help

Far more helpful would be, *"She was such a beautiful child."* –or– *"This is the hardest thing anyone could ever experience."* –or– *"This is too sad for words."*

What the heartbroken ones want is understanding. They rarely need noisy words. Here, more than anywhere, "weeping with the weeping" helps the most. Hugs, tears and conspicuous support, in the form of meals, calls and cards, are needed and God will do the fixing.

Recently President George W. Bush visited the areas in Southern California where 3500 homes had been destroyed by raging fires and 22 people lost their lives.

He said he wanted to comfort those who lost so much. But he admitted, *"All I can do is listen, hug, and be empathetic."* Our President showed a lot of understanding of the way comforting works. Listen. Hug. Empathize.

A hit and a miss

I was standing near some people when a man walked up. He said, *"Battery's dead—anybody got jumper cables?"* I was impressed when a woman spoke up: *"What a bummer. Sure, I've got cables in my trunk."* — **Bull's-eye!**

She acknowledged the crumminess of the situation first, then solved his problem. A tiny detail the guy may not have noticed at all, but, nevertheless, she slipped a little "hug" into his frustration. *("What a bummer.")* Three little words communicated empathy before fixing his problem.

> Joe was settling into his chair to watch golf on Saturday afternoon when he noticed something outside. *"Hey"*, he called out to his wife, *"the lawn guy missed the back yard."*
>
> *"Well, you better call him,"* she answered. — **Total miss!**

What his wife, Jennie, said was common sense—of the garden variety—that Joe did not appreciate. Her guidance missed the point. Joe needed a small dose of empathy. Jennie could have provided that with one word — "frustrating." Then Joe would have felt connected with Jennie, his feelings understood rather than ignored.

It was a tiny thing in Joe's life. It didn't hurt him at all in the grand scheme of things. Likewise, Jennie's response mattered little. But caring people work at such small things and develop a habit of dishing up those little words of compassion. I like to call them **verbal hugs**!

> Love suffers long and is kind;
> love does not envy;
> love does not parade itself,
> is not puffed up;
> does not behave rudely,
> does not seek its own,
> is not provoked,
> thinks no evil;
> does not rejoice in iniquity,
> but rejoices in the truth;
> bears all things,
> believes all things,

hopes all things,
endures all things.
I Corinthians 13: 4–7

In his book on I Corinthians 13, **"Love Within Limits"**, Lewis B. Smedes says this, regarding the words "love bears all things":

> *"Some of the most dramatic relief comes when someone enters our lives and accepts our burdens as his. When persons truly share in their spirit a consciousness of our hurt or loss, and thus carry our sorrow, they carry some of it away from us."*

In a wonderful story entitled **"The Porcupine Whose Name Didn't Matter"**, this kind of intimacy is demonstrated:

> One day, the Porcupine, who was a misfit and a castout in the forest society, stumbled across a Raccoon, blinded and near death from having been shot by a hunter. The Porcupine remained with the Raccoon for a long time and listened to him. When both fell silent, the Raccoon eventually asked, *"Are you still there?"* The Porcupine replied, *"Yes I'm still here. I was just wondering what to do now."*
>
> *"Oh, you don't have to do anything!"* said the dying Raccoon. *"Honestly, I mean that. Just stay with me for a little while. Just be there. Don't go away, please. I'm afraid. You wont go away will you?"* **The Way of the Wolf**, by Martin Bell

The Raccoon speaks for every hurting soul. That, finally, is what we want and need. Just "show up", talk little, shed our tears with the hurting, quietly hold them, pray personally, name their anguish and need.

This healing power of presence and being there is powerfully illustrated in **The Book of the Dun Cow** by Walter Wangerin. The Dun Cow comes to comfort the injured and grieving Chanticleer, the regal Rooster:

> "She put her soft nose against him, to nudge him into a more peaceful position. Gently she arranged his head so that he might clearly see her. Her sweet breath went into his nostrils…The Dun Cow took a single step back from the Rooster and looked at him…Her eyes were liquid with compassion—deep, deep, as the earth is deep. Her brow knew his suffering and knew, besides that, worlds more. But the goodness was that, though her brow knew so much, yet it bent over his pain alone and creased with it.
>
> Chanticleer watched his own desolation appear in the eyes of the cow, then sink so deeply into them that she shuddered. Her eyes pooled as she looked at him. The tears rose and spilled over…He watched—felt—the miracle take place. Nothing changed: The clouds would not be removed, nor his sons returned, nor his knowledge plenished. But there was this: his grief had become her grief, his sorrow her own. And though he grieved not one bit less for that, yet his heart made room for her, for her will and wisdom, and he bore the sorrow better."

The Dun Cow is more likely a metaphor for God than standard human caregiving. Nevertheless, the idea is clear and intends for us to be captured by that understanding of what true helping is like.

An ancient document asks, *"What is my only comfort in life and in death?"* The answer given goes like this: *"My only comfort is that I belong, body and soul, to my faithful savior Jesus Christ."* **Heidelberg Catechism**

Belonging is the comfort. To be part of someone who cares totally, like Jesus, is where comfort resides. When we duplicate shadows and fragments of that kind of care, we will be offering comfort.

This, of course, is what the Lord does. It is also what each of us can aspire to do. Usually it takes the form of "showing up" in difficult circumstances and listening to the laments, the details, the regrets, the shattered dreams, and everything else the stricken need to share. The closest formula there is for being a comforting friend is a caring presence — not a determination to fix things or to say cheering words, but an intention to be "walking with" the hurting.

Seldom is it words

Practically speaking, we should not "go off to comfort people with words." No, we reach out to them to show our oneness, our pain for them, our concern, our shared heartache. We show that we are part of them by hurting with them. If anything comforts, that does.

In forty years of working as a Pastor, I recall no one who told me that what helped most in the aftermath of a tragedy was something someone said to them. It always has been the meaningfulness of one's presence. The simple fact that they were present with evident compassion was the most meaningful medicine for their souls. One man recently talked about a friend who walked with him for hours. He cannot even recall who it was and certainly nothing that was said. It was the walking that helped.

Create a safe environment

The first care offered to anyone going through an emotional upset is just being present to the person in an accepting and interested way. First, we see to it that we are creating an environment of Care and Kindness that accepts, appreciates and allows whatever the other is feeling or thinking. We do not correct, trivialize, fix, distract or advise. If she needs to cry, we patiently let the crying happen. If she needs to walk, pound, or kick, we cooperate and join in as best we can. After that, we can go on to help her tell the story in factual detail, if that is what she wants to do. There is an emotional pressure in almost everyone who has been hit by a harsh life experience to tell all the details. A caring friend waits for that and patiently listens to the whole account— after she sees to it the hugs are delivered.

Ray Hommes' story shows in a remarkable way the power of helping another person to talk. His listening was crucial but in this case, while he heard it all, he understood only a few words. Nevertheless, the healing happened.

> After 2 years of language school, we still couldn't speak or understand Japanese very well. We moved into the house of a missionary family who were on furlough. We practiced our Japanese during those 6 months with the pastor of the church that was next to the house and also at an English center that we were involved with.
>
> One day, a member of the church, a college student, came to our house without any notice and knocked on our door. She stood there with another female student and announced, *"Hommes Sensei, you have to help my friend here because she is very depressed. She tried to take her life because*

she is having problems with her family, who live in the country." I told her to go into the church and wait in the lounge, and I would be with her shortly.

I quickly called the pastor on the phone (he lived about a half mile away) so that he could come over and we could both meet with the girls. When I called him, he didn't answer. I dreaded the thought that he might not be home. I waited for 5 more minutes and called again, but again there was no answer. I began to panic, but I knew I had to go next door to meet with them; there was no other option.

When I arrived, I told them that I had called the pastor, but he wasn't home. Then I sat down and saw that the friend of the church member was very downcast and tearful. I began with a word of prayer, and then I asked her what was happening in her life. She began to talk and cry and talk some more. She poured out her heart for about an hour and a half. (The Japanese language has a lot of words to describe feelings.) Then she began to settle down a bit, and I noticed that she was calmer. I closed with prayer, and both the girls left.

After the visit, I went next door to my wife and announced to her, with resignation, *"We're going back to Michigan!"* I hadn't understood 85% of what the girl was talking about; I had no idea of the content of the hour and a half conversation; and I was depressed. I had so hoped to be able use my counseling skills in the cross-cultural setting of Japan, but I was doubting it would ever happen. I didn't get much sleep that night.

The next afternoon there was a knock on our door. It was the church member who had come the day before with her suicidal friend. I was immediately swept with emotions of embarrassment and ineptness. She reached out and gave me a box of candy and a bouquet of flowers and said, *"Hommes Sensei, thank you so much for helping my friend yesterday. After you helped her, she decided to go home to her family, and she just called me a little while ago and told me that she has reconciled with her family and they are talking together, and she feels so much better. She doesn't want to take her life anymore"*

I looked at her like I was looking at a ghost! I thought to myself, "Are you talking to the right person?" Then she left, leaving me bewildered at the meaning of it all.

It wasn't until years later that I realized what had transpired there. I had "helped" her friend because I had <u>listened</u> to her, which is all that I could do. I had been listening to her very actively, however, looking intently for any non-verbal clues I could pick up and tones in her voice. She had been crying a lot, so I knew she was sad. Her posture was stooped over, so I knew she was despondent. But all I did was repeat at certain intervals statements like, *"It must be so hard or difficult or sad, etc."* And I said a lot of *"Ah, so desu ka"* replies, which mean, *"Oh, is that so."* It is basically an acknowledgement that you have heard the other person.

One thing I was so thankful for during the hour and a half was that she never asked me a question, which I would have recognized by the sound, *"ka,"* that is used to designate a question. If she had asked me a question, she would have known that I had not been understanding anything she had been talking about.

What I learned through this interaction is the power of active listening. There is definitely a strong power in listening to people who just need someone to give them their attention and to be understood. I sometimes wonder whether that experience was the reason why we ended up staying 19 years in Japan rather than returning to Michigan and feeling overwhelmed by the language and feeling incompetent to help people. There are not enough people around who are willing to take the time and energy needed to listen and let people talk about their feelings. Listening is a very powerful, underestimated force in helping and healing!

This is an incredible anecdote that proves better than most other examples the potent effectiveness of a caring presence.

Rejoice with those who rejoice

Another form of empathy, as scarce as any, is what we might call sharing another's joy. We talked earlier about Paul's advice about weeping. The first half calls us to **"weep with those who weep."** Those important words are now counterbalanced by **"rejoice with those who rejoice."** Surprisingly, as we consider these two profound bits of advice, we may conclude that it is easier to approach the brokenhearted with genuine tears of our own than to wholeheartedly be filled with joy when our neighbor discovers oil on his wilderness property, or experiences some other personal triumph.

Dancing for another's joy is hard

Tragedy triggers sympathy and compassion for hurting ones, but another's triumph often brings forth jealousy—a primal human fault so readily aroused. Truly dancing for joy when success pours down on a peer, but not on us, may call for a supernatural effort to override our envy.

It is sad to say, but another's loss can seemingly turn out to enhance our own condition. Therefore, approaching someone's calamity may not actually feel intimidating. But the windfall of good fortune, which is raining down on our neighbor, may turn the balance sheet of our life in a negative direction. "If he is getting ahead," we think, "then surely I am falling behind." I believe it is harder to rejoice with each other than to weep.

> Twenty-five years ago when our family lived in Michigan, my wife and I managed to squirrel away enough money to take a trip to Hawaii. We were so excited to be escaping our frigid state for the anticipated luxury of a week in "paradise". At the hospital where I worked, I discreetly mentioned the dream vacation that was a dozen days off.
>
> The reactions of friends were mostly "cognitive." That is, they would ask what island we were going to, or what airline we were booked on, how long we were going to be gone, etc. Decent questions. **All joyless!** Then Dr. Robert Baker responded with a hearty, *"Oh, hey, that's fantastic! What a great thing to do."* That

outburst tickled my soul deeply! Dr. Baker, that day, showed me how to celebrate with another person's good news. The others asked questions (perhaps disguising their jealousy) to show their interest; but the doctor **danced** with me.

The doctor read between the lines because I was not showing a lot of excitement about this expensive trip. I was a little self-conscious about it, maybe even apologetic; I did not seem to be dancing. He jumped behind the scenes and burst out with joy on my behalf. Often, that is what it takes.

Similarly, when Larry LaBonte scored a "hole-in-one" a while back, he did not rush in, shouting and rejoicing. Instead, he simply told us what had happened. It was up to us to start the celebration *for* him.

Pay attention

To rejoice with those who rejoice, we first have to pay attention. We need to hear their joy, even when it is delivered in a matter-of-fact or even monotonous tone.

A birth announcement of a grandchild may be told matter-of-factly, disguising the enormity of thanksgiving held in check by a modest new grandfather. A proper, loving reaction calls for boisterous congratulations and hearty slaps on the back—behavior way beyond what the new grandpa himself exhibits.

Strike up the band

Modesty describes most folks. So when they "hit the jackpot," ordinary human beings quietly send up their fireworks with only a small circle of intimates. Beyond that, triumphs, accomplishments, and victories only leak out and are quietly played down. It is for these that we must develop a finely tuned antenna to hear the big news the way it should be heard and strike up the band for a proper celebration.

Recently, I shyly showed a friend a photo of a large sign in front of a bookstore. My cautious approach came from the fact that the sign displayed, in prominent letters, an announcement that included my name and that I would be signing books in the store on the coming weekend. My reluctant attitude came from experience that has taught me the risk of flaunting one's accomplishments. Sure enough, the response was a slight mocking, *"Oh, we have a celebrity in our midst."* I immediately regretted taking the photograph out of my pocket. I had wanted to share the tickle I felt, but the needling reminded me how difficult it is to **share** joys.

Big-headedness rarely happens

In the same vein, upon learning of the publication of a book I had labored hard on, another friend counseled that she sure hoped my success didn't go to my head. She thought she was acknowledging a successful venture, but there was little joy-sharing trickling out of her warning. Human beings carry an almost ineradicable illusion in their core that success or a successful venture makes one arrogant. It doesn't happen. Therefore, no matter who or what the accomplishment, the victory, the promotion or the acquisition, the person needs the caring, wholehearted celebration or congratulations of bystanders and friends.

Exaggerate!

No one is too small or insignificant to bring that kind of gift. Exaggerate! Stretch beyond your usual comfort level in expressing appreciation and giving congratulations on another's behalf. If you do not genuinely feel the feelings, act like you do. The feelings will grow inside you. It is better to act your way to the right feelings than to wait for the feelings before acting.

Share victories

When hearts break, the need for support shouts clearly. Hard as it may be, caring people reach out to give support and encouragement; they know that support is needed. Accomplishments, however, do not cry out in the same way. Those who are gifted in lovely ways or are champions and winners do not look needy—do not seem to need support. They may even appear to be above the rest of us—or so it seems. But a caring community grows stronger when victories are shared and celebrated together. And the joyous—shy and modest as they may be—connect more solidly when rejoicers reach past the surface and embrace them with joy.

Some say that the hardest part of tragic circumstances is the loneliness of the journey. But those who move into joyous achievements say the same. Rare, they claim, are those who see and share their joy at a level that resonates positively. Accurately tuning into another's good news is a fine art. Both ends of the scale—tragedy or triumph—open up opportunities for caring folks to walk alongside. Sometimes they weep and sometimes they dance!

Back to the bad stuff . . .

God lifts people up after they have been knocked down. Even those hit by the most tragic conditions imaginable gradually emerge, get up again, laugh, love and dance once more. God does it. People watch it. St. Paul puts it this way, which testifies to that unfailing healing presence of God:

> We are hard pressed on every side,
> but not crushed;

Perplexed, but not in despair;
Persecuted, but not abandoned;
Struck down, but not destroyed.
II Corinthians 4: 8, 9

A few years after a drunk driver killed his wife and three little children, Robert Trueblood's golden laughter again filled every room he entered. Although the pain in his heart would never be gone, God had brought a new wife, Diane, and new children into his life. God lifted him to his feet and filled him once more with joy.

Clyda Holbrook's husband was murdered before her eyes and she was brutally stabbed and left for dead. Clyda today says, *"My cup runneth over."* She glows with energy and vitality. God has restored her soul.

God heals. We walk alongside as the healing happens.

If we could accomplish one thing in our present world in regard to human suffering, it would be to eliminate both those who stay away and those intent on fixing people. Both extremes hurt and make hard things worse.

What we all need is for people to share with us what we are going through as best they can, whether it be either joy or sorrow. We need friends who will shout for joy when we are ecstatic or experiencing triumph. We need friends who will cry out for us when we are knocked down, and cry out to God on our behalf. God takes care of the healing, but we need friends, who are full of care, surrounding us while the restoration is underway. Let God do it God's way while we walk along side.

JUST WALK WITH ME

I have a problem. I want to tell you about it.
No, I really don't. I'd rather keep it to myself;

handle it alone. I do think it would be good for me to share it with you though, I don't want to because I'm afraid of what you'll say or how you'll act.

I'm afraid you might feel sorry for me in a way that makes me feel pathetic. Like I'm some "poor thing."

I'm afraid you will try to cheer me up. That you will give me words or texts or prayers that tell me in a subtle way to stop feeling bad. If you do that, I'll feel worse (but hide it behind my obedient, cheerful smile). I'll feel you don't understand. I'll feel you are making light of my problem (if it can be brushed away with some brief words of cheer.)

I'm afraid you'll give me an answer. That this problem I've been wrestling with for some time now and about which I have thought endless thoughts will be belittled. You can answer in a half-minute what I've struggled with for weeks?

I'm afraid, also, you might ignore my problem, talk quickly about other things, tell me of your own.

I'm afraid, too, you might see me stronger than I am; not needing you to listen and care. (It's true I can get along alone, but I shouldn't.)

What I'd really like is if you would "just walk with me". Listen as I begin in some blundering, clumsy way to break through my fearfulness of being exposed as weak. Hold my hand and pull me gently as I falter and begin to draw back. Say a word, make a motion, or a sentence that says, "I'm with you." If you've been where I am, tell me how you felt in a way that I can know you're trying to walk with me—not change me.

But I'm afraid...

...you'll think I'm too weak to deserve respect and responsibility.

...you'll explain what's happening to me with labels and interpretations.

Or you'll ask me, "What are you going to do about it?"

PLEASE just walk with me.

All those other things seem so much brighter and sharper, smarter and expert. But what really takes love is to "Just Walk With Me".

I'm sure what I want is for people to have the Good Shepherd as their model. People, who in their own way, bring to others an experience of:

> The Lord is my Shepherd
> I shall not want....
> Yes, even when I walk
> Through the valley...
> You're with me (walking with Me)
> **Psalm 23**

Discussion questions for Chapter 6 are on pages 238–243.

Kindness Example

Joan Winter's neighbor was dying and visitors were limited to family only. Joan decided to make a banner that the man could read from his window. The neighbors gathered and imprinted their handprints on a plastic shower curtain, along with words wishing him well. He enjoyed the banner the remaining days of his life and his wife placed it prominently on the pulpit at the church when they gathered for the Memorial Service.

Reflection: Here was a very serious situation, lightened up by an enjoyable project that brought joy to a dying man. Everybody needs to know that they are cared for and remembered.

๛๛๛๛๛๛๛

Kindness Example

My friend Phil Phillips' hands shake some; he is in the
early stages of Parkinson's Disease. The tremors in his
hands seem to be a turn-off to some he meets in the day's
activities. In banks, stores and elsewhere, the clerks and
others from time to time communicate negative reactions to
Phil because of the shaking hands. They will then treat him
curtly, rudely at times and, clearly, with less respect. They
react as if he is dangerous, or a drug user or some other
character worthy of disdain.

Since this reaction is not rare, The Parkinsons Advocacy
Group has printed small yellow cards the patient can carry
in his wallet. The card can then be handed to those he
perceives as being unkind or rude, and hopefully the
recipient will rethink his attitude and behavior. Here, in
part, is what the card says:

> *I am not under the influence of alcohol, nor am
> I mentally ill. I have Parkinson's Disease. It is
> not contagious…it is a movement disorder.*

The card is stunningly effective, Phil says. After reading it,
behavior changes 180 degrees. Suddenly they see a
person—not a threat, and they treat him as they should.

Reflection: How easy it is to stereotype people on the basis of
some unimportant mannerism, appearance or trait. Followers
of Jesus, and everyone else as well, should not have to read a
card to turn on respect when someone's hands shake.

Kindness Example

While standing in line at the IMAX theatre in Los Angeles, I witnessed an exceptionally kind confrontation. In front of us, a family with two kids waited. Immediately in front of them, a middle aged man began to light up a cigarette. As the cigarette was being lit, the couple behind him looked at each other. They both frowned as the initial cloud of smoke drifted their way.

Then the frowning man made a move. Exchanging his frown for a smile, he tapped the smoker on the shoulder and said, *"I will save your place in line if you would be willing to step away a little to enjoy your cigarette."* The surprised smoker quickly accepted the invitation. With a smile, he moved away and everybody around witnessing the drama smiled with appreciation.

Reflection: Confrontation does not have to be heated. Here it was gentle and very effective. Everybody won. It just took a little self-care and concern for his wife for the confronter to generate an idea. Chances are that he gave a welcome gift to the smoker who wanted the smoke but was trapped in the line.

Pro-active care satisfies a lot of needs. But it takes a little courage to break out of your comfort zone and suggest or negotiate with another. It takes a dose of courage we often are afraid to muster. Then no one is helped.

споспоспоспосп

-7-

A Daily Diet of
Care and Kindness

One day Linda, my wife, said, *"We ought to have a checklist to carry or post on the refrigerator for the special acts of Care and Kindness we deliver every day."*

She went on with the idea of keeping score. "We are taught from childhood on up to pray daily, watch our language, eat the right food, and to be careful of our appearance. But we are not programmed constantly to show thoughtfulness, encouragement and loving kindness to those around us everywhere we go."

Keep daily score

We need to take inventory daily on how well we have done that day, was her point. It is a stunningly good idea. Her observations slammed home the shortage of consistent emphasis on this central need. Care and Kindness is not consciously downplayed, but it certainly is not high on the daily menu of what followers of Jesus should be thinking about.

Help yourself

There are two important things about Care and Kindness. The first is that a life-style that shows compassion and concern for others helps the one delivering such goods. It is good for one's health to be consistently kind and intentionally compassionate. Depression is lifted, one's own spirit is brightened, and one's whole physical system is enhanced by giving to another.

Heal others

Secondly, and logically connected, is that those who receive Care and Kindness are healthier when their spirits are lifted by kindness and encouragement. When people are shown that they are appreciated and cared for, their physical bodies respond with greater vitality. This was first proven ages ago when babies in orphanages were found to be fading into death from the absence of being held and touched.

Our lives are purposeful. We are placed here to create heaven on earth. Originally, we had Paradise. Now we are called to rebuild. We are participants with God in bringing to humankind the goodness, justice, beauty, security, peace and love that is fully known in heavenly places. That is our purpose in life.

All our educational concerns, even our recreation, have but one aim—to be God's people, knowledgeable, skilled, compassionate, and contributing to the growth and improvement of life on earth. That is called Kingdom Building. For some, it is done with hammer and nails; for others, it is done with teaching, discovering, creating, maintaining, growing, producing. Every effort of humanity is supposed to be purposefully contributing to the betterment of life for the whole human race. Therefore, it should be part of our daily agenda.

Train the children

As most children raised in Christian homes are encouraged daily to say their prayers, and clean their plates, we want them schooled in doing good works every day. We desire that a mother will ask as a child is put to bed, *"Did you help someone today? Were you kind and considerate of your classmates today? Can you give me a special example of Care and Kindness you performed?"*

This child will reach maturity, not only remembering to say her prayers daily, but to do an inventory of the intentional kindness she sprinkled about in her day.

We pay a lot of attention to taking care of our bodies. Diet and exercise are central ingredients of everyone's consciousness. Let's add another item: in addition to the foods we eat, the workouts we engaged in, the devotions we absorb, how about counting the daily acts of intentional Care and Kindness that go beyond our ordinary politeness and etiquette? Let's bring up our children to regard no day as complete without checking off the special efforts of Care and Kindness extended.

To do this well calls for adults to model such living. Sincere followers of Jesus often long to hear God speak to them personally. Others wait to feel the presence of God in their lives. Some hear God or feel God's touch. Some experience inner warmth they know to be God's presence. But most human beings do not hear or feel God other than through the reading of Scripture.

But, more important than hearing or feeling, we are called to express God in our lives. It is our calling to be Godlike in our lives, to let the goodness of God flow through us in simple acts of Care and Kindness, rather than longing for a special contact from God.

Concern for the well-being of others, is a primary issue in living as a follower of Jesus. Steady, quiet trust in the Lord is a wonderful way to live. Secure faith that stands firm in the storms of life is an admirable achievement—a universally admired virtue. But is such unwavering faith, such unshakeable trust, the goal of Christian living?

The Apostle James implies that more is expected:

> Religion that God our Father accepts
> as pure and faultless is this—
> to look after orphans and
> widows in their distress
> and to keep oneself
> from being polluted by the world.
> **James 1:27**

In summarizing this thought, we see that support and encouragement of any and all struggling souls is what true religion is about. Everyone is called to this task. Jesus said it this way:

> You are the light of the world…
> let your light shine before others,
> that they may see your good deeds
> and praise your father in heaven.
> **Matthew 5:14–16**

Belief needs to be expressed. It must be demonstrated! "Faith without works is dead," again quoting James. That means that being a child of God requires showing loving kindness to the world. It calls for behaving in uniquely gracious ways all the time.

Excellence of work

Our daily work must be excellent. We are called to fine craftsmanship, immaculate bookkeeping, thoughtful delivery of goods and services. Science, sales, transportation, electronics—all the occupations we are engaged in contribute to Kingdom building in the sense of bringing greater harmony, satisfaction, health and God-glorifying happiness to this earth.

It takes any number of forms as we use our gifts and talents to responsibly create a better world as teachers, truckers, financial planners, computer programmers, assessors, mapmakers and all other vocations in which we find ourselves. All our efforts and responsibilities are part of our marching orders from Jesus to be Kingdom Builders.

The rest of the story

There is more. Something more than well-done daily work is needed. The human race needs our simple, regular, thoughtful acts of Care and Kindness. Followers of Jesus are obliged to be the conscientious deliverers of this loving kindness. It may be above and beyond our daily vocational challenges or it may be wrapped up in our daily work.

Cornelius Plantinga reflects on the attitude of the powerful early American preacher, Jonathan Edwards:

> According to Edwards, the way to tell whether we have been truly born again by the Spirit of God is to see whether we have a godly practice. Do we have in our lives a pattern of good works governed by the Ten Commandments and other Biblical guides? Do we make good deeds our central business, the way a physician makes medicine her central business. And do we keep on in our practice of godliness for the long run of our lives and not just for little spurts while other people are watching? *"The Christian's Central Business"*, in **The Banner** 1-21-02

As was said earlier, there is personal payoff in making Care and Kindness the central business of your life. Not only are we doing what is right, needed, and good for others—it helps us, too. Care and Kindness diets make the participant healthier. It is a known fact that speaking words of encouragement, and appreciation, showing compassion to someone who is hurting, patting a youngster on the back, sending out a smile, giving a caring touch, not only lifts the recipient's spirits but heals the one who offers such goodness as well.

An unexpected prescription

Here is what one of our country's most famous psychiatrists, Karl Menninger, said when fielding a question from an audience after a lecture on mental health. The question was, *"What would you advise a person to do if that person felt a nervous breakdown coming on?"* Most expected him to say, *"Consult a psychiatrist."*

To their astonishment, he replied, *"Lock up your house, go across the railroad tracks, find someone in need and do something to help that person."* Obviously he was touting the health benefits of doing good to a soul in need.

Norman Vincent Peale declared this about the benefits of Care and Kindness:

> So deep and meaningful is the joy and the enthusiasm that is born in one's mind and heart by human love and helpfulness that it has the power to motivate for a lifetime...

> You don't have to be a doctor to say or do that which puts light in a human eye and joy in a human face. Simply practice Jesus' commandment that we love one another.

Go out and do something for somebody. These are the things that make happy people. Here is the one never-failing source of joy and enthusiasm we are all talking about.

Look to Jesus

Positive living takes thought, energy and belief. The primary source of power for any form of positive giving is Jesus. In Jesus we have a powerful motivating source for daily living that endeavors to spread good will and good deeds everyday. Jesus' life, teaching, and presence is the motivating fuel for this kind of living. Looking to Jesus reminds us when we get bogged down in our personal ventures too much. When we look to Jesus, we see the ultimate expression of God's love. Jesus' abuse, his rejection, the scourging and mockery he took, and finally his death on the cross, are the ultimate expression of God's loving kindness and our primary motivation as His Spirit energizes us. His Resurrection reminds us that when we die for others by giving of our time, energy, love and attention, we will be restored, renewed, revived by the same power that raised Jesus from the grave.

We are called to generate sacrificial living for others

Sacrificial living is often uncomfortable and may even cause suffering for ourselves. We are called to take risks for others—to die to our personal comfort zone a little in order to express the love of God in our lives.

This means looking constantly to extend healing and vitality to others, at some cost to ourselves. Often it calls us to inconvenience, to discomfort. It calls us to sacrifice our time or energy and run the risk of mistake making.

It is this easy

People need us to brighten their lives. Sometimes, a brightened life is like a resurrected life. Encouragement, loving kindness and appreciation can lift a morbid spirit in a surprising way. A Ministry Associate Training student of mine gave this report:

> "At the checkout at Sav-On's, I had the opportunity to get to know the checker, Heather. Seeing that I was buying cat food, she knew I owned a cat. This prompted her to tell me that she had a cat also and that he had been seriously wounded the week before from an unknown animal bite. I responded *'How awful!'* These simple words allowed her to continue to share all her concerns for her favorite pet. Simply listening to her fears and concerns seemed to help her. I was amazed how two words on my part could be so beneficial."

Two words, and then staying to listen. No obvious pain, just polite considerateness.

Resurrection, renewal, rehabilitation works in our lives too. Our own dying is complemented by new life that follows our suffering, be the distress ever so slight.

People are spiritual, intertwined with a physical body

Today Linda, my wife, is in her tenth post-surgery day. Her convalescence will extend several more weeks, even though she is home, up and around. Our adult Sunday School class has provided a series of wonderful meals, brought in to our house, so we are doing very well. It wasn't just food. It was love and concern. More than that, they brought strong doses of healing. The food was wrapped in the vitamins of Care and Kindness, contributing significantly to Linda's recovery. Lonely, neglected, worried ones do not heal nearly as smoothly as the loved.

Kind words alter body chemistry

Whisper a kind word into someone's ear and you will initiate an improvement in his or her health. Such a gift is not just sound waves that land in the auditory canal and enter the receptive center of the brain. Kind words are not just pleasantries that tickle us. They do that, plus impact the chemistry of the body. Kind words are like a shot of spirit-lifting vitamins that go through the whole person, making them healthier.

> Anxiety in the heart...
> causes depression,
> but a kind word makes it glad.
> **Prov 12:25**

> Pleasant words are like a honeycomb,
> Sweetness to the soul and health to the bones
> **Prov 16:24**

A few years ago, a research program on Cardiac patients who had damaged hearts and no predictable possibility of recovery, turned up something surprising. As the clinicians studied the miles of EKG printouts, they found islands of health in the sick hearts of those being studied.

Damaged and weakened hearts, beating irregularly, spasmodically, faintly, and/or operating on defective cardiac systems, every once in a while looked healthy according to the EKG printout, and the researchers wanted to find out how this could be.

Touch heals, too

Because every minute of the EKG had a time printed on it, they were able to go back to see what was going on with the patient at that moment of his hospital situation. Their painstaking efforts yielded surprising results. They discovered that most often, when there was an island of health on the EKG printout, the patient was being cared for by nursing staff in some hands-on kind of way. They were being touched, and the touch, plus the presence of personal care, normalized their broken hearts for a few seconds.

This study was one of many that show that the human person is not just a simple mechanical machine. For many decades we have been leaning more and more to that idea about the body. Fed by scientific achievements, discoveries and wonders, we have begun to believe that the human system is totally physical and the answers to breakdowns and malfunctions are all to be found in laboratories, medicines, surgeries and other medical solutions. Thirty years ago, Jerome Frank, an eminent M.D. at Johns Hopkins Medical Center, said, *"It is clear now that science is a Pied Piper, luring humanity down the path to destruction by dazzling it with endless goodies."* He was saying we put too much trust in science. That was thirty years ago.

The laughter lesson

The most famous statement against the sheer physicality of human beings came from a writer, Norman Cousins. Mr. Cousins had been diagnosed with an ailment having no known cure. He decided to fight back by supplementing conventional medical treatment with daily doses of laughter. He had a hunch that feeling better through laughter might help his entire system. He managed the laughter diet by watching comedies on video tape at least an hour a day.

Norman Cousins achieved his goal. The regimen of medicine and laughter defeated the supposedly unbeatable illness and he became a sought after consultant in the medical world. His thesis was that dispirited people are vulnerable to illness and they need their spirits lifted to overcome their illness. Laughter is spirit lifting and a heightened spirit makes the whole body healthier.

The EKG discovery and the laughter experiment suggest something very big that Christians have forgotten to a great extent. These discoveries point out that the human being is more than narrowly mechanical. There is something more, which when properly nourished, makes a difference in the physical. I call it the spiritual dimension. The Lord created men and women as living souls, not as just living bodies. The living soul includes the body, but is much more. The living soul concept is about the spirituality of the human race.

People are more than physical

The Care and Kindness campaign is established on the foundation that human beings are spiritual/physical unities. People are psychosomatic, that is, body/spirit. The spiritual is intertwined with the physical. A blow to the physical system always affects one's spirit as well. The broken body is often accompanied by a wounded spirit. At the same time, an inspired soul helps the physical person recover or stay healthier, and a physically cared for body enables the spirit to thrive.

Care and Kindness is about lifting the spirits of those we know and meet. Such encounters are made with the confidence that such infusions of loving-kindness are health giving, not just a nice thing to do. This Care and Kindness project rises out of the conviction that every follower of Jesus Christ has an opportunity and a responsibility to contribute to the health and well-being of our planet. It is accomplished by daily distribution of Care and Kindness to those we meet. In doing this, we are living, breathing antidotes to the spirit-depleting experiences every human being is dealing with, both the minor and the major kinds. The losses, setbacks, terrors, threats and dangers, both real and imagined, are spiritual infections that need to be opposed. Care and Kindness carries that healing potion.

> I interrupted my writing today to run a few errands. One stop was at the drive-up mailbox to drop off a few letters. When I arrived, there was a car parked a few yards ahead of the mail slot, preventing me from driving up to where I needed to be. I was upset as I noticed someone sitting in the car fiddling with something. I was very irritated. Then the car door opened and a middle aged woman got out and started walking back to the mail drop.

> My window was open and I considered scolding her. Instead, I decided to give her a big smile. The troubled look on her face was instantaneously erased. She smiled back and apologized. I think I healed her, or at least gave her a shot of fresh joy that lifted her mood and strengthened her body.

Loss batters the Spirit

When the Biblical character named Job was blasted by one enormous loss after another, he said, "My spirit is broken." Then he spoke about the dire results of his broken spirit. He laments: "My days are extinct. The grave is ready for me." In the same context Job says: "My eye has grown dim from grief and my arms and legs are wasting away."

His spirit is battered by grief. His losses are destroying his spiritual strength. He expects to die as he sees his health undermined and his body weakening. Grief is an affliction of the human spirit that needs healing. Today we know that careful attention to the needs of a grieving person is necessary so that they can recover. We also know that widowed persons do not have strong health records following the loss of a spouse. Their loss so devastates their spirit that they become ill and even die. They need the spirit-healing medicine of Care and Kindness.

There are costly biochemical effects within us from the spiritual blows to our systems. Broken bones, life-threatening diseases, pain, loss of work, death of loved ones—all sock our souls bluntly. Fear, panic, dread, despair, depression, hate and rage drain us of health. At the same time hope, will to live, faith, confidence, cheerfulness and laughter play a vital part in restoring the body. These positive spiritual commodities are biochemical replenishers that help those knocked down to recover. The deliverers of these vitamins are in large part women and men who enter another's life with love and care, understanding and concern.

Norman Cousins said, "There is little doubt that fear is a great accelerator of disease. Conversely, hope, faith, confidence and the will to live set an auspicious stage for efforts toward recovery."

Love heals

Bernie Siegel, author of **Love, Medicine and Miracles**, says, "I feel that all disease is ultimately related to a lack of love...The truth is: love heals."

Walter Lippman, a political commentator, long ago wrote of what love does to people: "Their whole activity is energized and victorious. They walk better, their digestion improves, they think more clearly, their secret worries drop away, the world is fresh and interesting and they can do more than they dreamed they could."

Forgiveness heals

Jesus, at times, would heal people with the promise "your sins are forgiven". Imagine that! His point seemed to be that the physical problem was connected to spiritual issues. "Your sins are forgiven" is a powerful spiritual gift if taken in and embraced. It has the potential, obviously, to so bless the person that his spirit unlocks the healing of the physical challenge.

Here is the exact situation where Jesus used that approach:

> Some men brought to him a paralytic,
> lying on a mat.
> When Jesus saw their faith,
> he said to the paralytic,
> 'Take heart, son; your sins are forgiven'...
> and the man got up and went home.
> **Matthew 9:2**

The Psalms and the Proverbs are filled with the connection between spiritual well-being and physical health. The Psalms are eloquent about how those who live carefully, trusting God and obeying God's precepts, will be blessed with physical health and well-being.

> Blessed is the man...
> whose delight is in the laws of the Lord,
> and on his law he meditates day and night.
> He is like a tree planted by streams of water
> which yields its fruit in season
> and whose leaf does not wither.
> Whatever he does prospers.
> **Psalm 1**

The Proverbs give us some more personally practical guidelines that promise to make a difference in our general health. Proverbs builds a strong case for the interdependence of the spirit and the body. For example:

Do not be wise in your own eyes;
fear the Lord and shun evil.
This will bring health to your body and
nourishment to your bones.
Proverbs 3:7–8

A happy heart makes the face cheerful,
but heartache crushes the spirit.
Proverbs 15:13

A cheerful heart is good medicine,
But a crushed spirit dries up the bones.
Proverbs. 17:22

A heart at peace gives life to the body,
but envy rots the bones.
Proverbs 14:30

A man's spirit sustains him in sickness, but a
crushed spirit who can bear?
Proverbs 18:14

Each Proverb in its own way implies that the issues of a person's life that we call spiritual are not isolated pieces of their lives but are intertwined with physical health in some way. Therefore the campaign to ignite passion for spreading loving kindness is a drive for health-enhancing through spirit-lifting.

Human beings are spiritual beings inhabiting a physical body. Spiritual well-being is the number one concern for each of us as we endeavor to be productive, creative, responsible followers of Jesus. We must care for people and about people, because through Care and Kindness, we strengthen the whole person, spiritually and physically.

People need people

Jesus said, "Where two or three are gathered in My name, there I am present." These words are also a prescription for health. They say that we are more likely to be touched, nourished, embraced by God in Jesus when we are with other people in worship, study, prayer, fellowship, or recreation. That is when Jesus' Holy Spirit is most effective: healing our brokenness and picking up the struggling.

Along that same line of thinking, Lewis Smedes says,

> "Personal communion is what the image of God is about. Biblical revelations tell us to stop thinking about ourselves as isolated islands of rational God-likeness and think of ourselves instead as coming into real humanity when we live in genuine, personal fellowship with others. A single person is the image of God, but he is God's image only when he personally relates in love to others."
> **Sex for Christians**, Lewis Smedes

Wholeness is enhanced by being in communion with other people. Alone, we are not complete. Alone, we are not spiritually strengthened in the way necessary to experience whole-person health and well-being. People need people because the presence of God works effectively in the arena of people caring about each other.

The Prayer of St. Francis

Lord, make me an instrument of your peace.
Where there is hatred, let me sow love;
Where there is injury, pardon;
Where there is despair, hope;

Where there is darkness, light;
Where there is sadness, joy.;

O Divine Master, grant that I may not
So much seek to be consoled as to console;
To be understood as to understand;
To be loved as to love;
For it is in giving that we receive;
It is in pardoning that we are pardoned;
And it is in dying
That we are born to eternal life.

Discussion questions for Chapter 7 are on pages 243–246.

Kindness Example

When Jim Jameson's glasses were lost, nobody took the loss very seriously. After all, Jim was in Hospice care. Since time was running out on his life, the prevailing attitude was that his glasses weren't necessary.

Earl Howe thought differently. He hustled around until new glasses were crafted for Jim. Jim was delighted that he could again watch TV, and see his family and visitor's faces.

I remember visiting a 103 year old woman once and found her reading a novel. It struck me as an important lesson: people are alive and can value pleasure, adventure, beauty, until their last breath. Earl Howe realized this when he saw to it that Jim Jameson was equipped again for the pleasures of life, even though his physical life was ending.

Reflection: It is so easy to reduce folks, on the basis of their looks or their diagnosis. The very aged, especially, can be dehumanized because of their bodily weakness and sagging attractiveness. The very sick can be neglected because it appears they don't have long to live.

There is no point at which we can treat another as less than a fully deserving, precious child of God. There is no point where we can disregard another's need for thoughtful care and consideration—like with Jim Jameson's spectacles.

ﻬﻬﻬﻬﻬﻬ

Kindness Example

Carolyn Harmes stopped for the red light at Lewis and
Memory Lane. Off to one side, she noticed an old woman
struggling. She had dropped some groceries and was not
doing well gathering them up off the street. Quickly,
Carolyn slammed her gearshift into PARK, jumped from
the car, rushed over and solved the problem. Then she
raced back and still got back in the driver's seat before the
light turned green.

Reflection: A split-second decision and then success!
How easy it would have been to feel like it couldn't be
done and let the possibility of another driver being delayed
keep her from Care and Kindness. Happens often!

ৡৡৡৡৡৡ

Kindness Example

Lance Armstrong, Tour de France champion bike racer, pedaling at top speed was dropped to the pavement by the protruding handle of a yellow bag in the hands of a spectator who had leaned into the riding lanes. Immediately, his closest pursuers, even the one who trailed by only fifteen seconds, slowed to wait for Lance to pick himself up, dust himself off, and get back on his bike. Then they all took off again with fierce competitive determination to defeat each other.

Reflection: What a reassuring protocol in a world where winning at all costs seems to be the rule! In the Tour de France, courtesy still lives. When the most intense competitors we know show that kind of consideration, the whole world wakes up a little. The ripples of fair-play and kinship spread around the globe when such noble behavior is exhibited.

The Tour De France story has a strong kinship to a report from a Special Olympics event. A Down's Syndrome foot racer had stumbled and fell on her face. There too, instead of taking advantage of her fall, all the other runners stopped, helped her up, saw she was okay, and then resumed the race.

The Special Olympics has no rule calling for stopping to help the fallen as the Tour De France does. For those youngsters, their concern was instinctive. Isn't this the Spirit of Christ coming through? Perhaps many of us have covered that kind of compassion with unbridled competitiveness.

ଓଜଓଜଏଜଏଜ

-8-

Generous Giving May Be A Sign Of Humility

Here is an example of humble behavior, written by a MAT (Ministry Associate Training) student who was seriously working at being intentionally kind and caring:

> I had to go into a store I detest. And the people there were true to form—rude. I did not allow this to deter me as I greeted each worker in my path with a 'good afternoon' and thanked the checker with *"I would like to thank you for your patience and courtesy in what appears to be a very busy day for you."* She responded with an impolite *"yeah, its always busy around here."*

> The student then summarized with, *"Well, I don't know that this all went well, but I tried."*

The word "humble" conjures up mental images, most of which are not attractive. We see timid, shy folks, with self-deprecating mannerisms that say, "Don't look at me, I am nothing." When we label someone humble, it usually implies she or he follows along quietly and passively, making no waves, taking no risks, unlike the person above who spoke her greetings and presented her compliment, in spite of an unwelcoming environment. Seldom is a dynamic leader regarded as humble. We do not often regard someone who freely hands out words of appreciation or steps up and congratulates winners as demonstrating humility. Most minds think that assertive behavior usually <u>cancels</u> humility.

Humility defined correctly

This standard notion of humility needs re-defining. Humility may better be seen as "the capacity and willingness to do what needs to be done". Rather than seeing it as mannerisms, or the way a person looks, humility has to do with one's capacity to move into places where help is needed to step forward and offer something.

The basic definition of the word may include "not thinking of yourself as greater than others." But this would not call for trying to look a certain way, or to appear abashed, like you had no confidence. The fact is that the humble folks may look very confident and self-assured, even if they are not.

Pride disguised as humility

Think about this: It is more likely to be pride than humility that causes one to hang back, look shy, act reserved, keep one's thoughts, ideas and questions to oneself. What we often regard as sweet humbleness may in fact be cool self-centeredness. A reluctance to speak or step forward may in fact be fear of how others think of us, wanting to avoid being regarded as bold or wrong or brash. That's self-centered-ness, disguised as the opposite—disguised as humble self-abasement. Being careful so that no one misunderstands you is not humility. It is selfish egocentrism.

The truly humble are not excessively preoccupied with self and having to look good or appear humble. They are characterized by seeing what is needed and then stepping forward to try to meet the need. This is because humility looks at what can be done and does not worry about appearances.

A humble person can ask "dumb questions". He doesn't have to already know everything. He dares to ask a person's name when he has forgotten it, rather than act as if he knows it. He is willing to ask about delicate issues, like a death in the family, even if others avoid such topics. He mentions the smudge on another's face instead of letting it stay there.

Jesus was humble. He didn't withhold himself. He stepped up to meet the needs of humanity at great cost to himself. He gave what he had, rather than be concerned about protecting his reputation or his skin. He walked away when there was need sometimes, because he was tired. He was not controlled by public opinion. He confronted a woman's unseemly marital history instead of winking at it.

The humble are bold
Jesus spoke up courageously, and at other times remained silent when he could have benefited his safety by speaking. Sometimes he was furious and it was obvious. There were occasions when he was let down and disappointed and he said so to his disciples.

Humility is necessary to boldly face evil because humbleness is the willingness to fight what needs opposition, rather than being concerned with simply protecting oneself. There is a time to speak and a time to be still. Humility weighs the challenge and makes a choice to do one or the other.

I once asked a group for a volunteer to play the piano for our opening devotions. No one moved. Finally I saw a nudge and a young woman was coaxed forward. She played superbly. Why had she resisted? I assume she felt that was the humble way to act. Reluctance was regarded as pious and gracious. But she was mistaken. Humility is stepping forward when there is a need—ignoring public opinion.

> A seminary student explained to me that his gifts for ministry did not include visiting in hospitals. He wanted to be excused from that duty. He was not excused and proved to be rather effective at this kind of work. He admitted later that his reserve was based on his concern about looking weak in this bedside ministry.

This is a common condition. Those who fear looking bad neglect much care to the wounded or grieving. But humble folks move in anyway.

Humility and Care and Kindness

When it comes to Care and Kindness, those who spread such goodness are the humble. Everyone carries a reservoir of positive thoughts, reactions and impressions. Smiles, touch, compliments, appreciation, and encouragement are part of each of us. They, who distribute such gifts, giving of their time and energy to bless others, are humble people. They risk rebuff or embarrassment by greeting strangers. They give gifts to those who are expecting nothing. They praise those who can give little in return. They even reward with kind words those who have everything. They resist staying in their comfort zone so that they can reach out to others. That is what humility looks like.

We must grow in awareness of the universal and unquenchable thirst for love. Then, as we diminish in our reserve and self-consciousness, we become more humble. If we sprinkle, spread and send encouragement, appreciation, kindness, support and blessings to those we meet and know, we become more humble.

The more we give, the better our world will be and we in turn may reap the bountiful rewards of having our own spirit lifted.

So consider what is needed. Realize the hunger and thirst for affirmation in every living soul. Step up and give what you have been keeping inside. Boldly! Obediently! Then you are a humble soul.

What about receiving?

Humble, assertive giving bumps into the fine art of receiving. "It is better to give than to receive," Scripture says. But learning to graciously accept a gift is another evidence of spiritual maturity.

When my Dad, The Reverend Gareth S. Kok, was in his late nineties, he had developed the habit of saying, *"What?"* any time you told him something. So invariably, every thing we said had to be repeated. We got used to it. His advanced age gave him the right to this small idiosyncrasy we attributed to failing hearing. I'd routinely say, *"It is a nice day."* *"What?"* he would reply. And I was ready to say again, *"It's a nice day."*

One day, as I sat at a table with him and some other gentlemen residents at Artesia Christian Home, one of them said to me, *"Your dad was a great preacher."* Immediately, my Dad reached his hand to the man and said, *"Thank you."* There was no need for a repeat of this compliment. He didn't say "what?" He heard it the first time and enjoyed it greatly at age 98. Nearing one hundred years of age, he still greatly relished a compliment and accepted it with grace.

When offered a gift, the reactions of those who are receiving differ. Some are gracious and comfortable receivers. Some radiate appreciation in lovely ways. There are many, however, who have difficulty accepting acts of kindness. Either they do not recognize the gift for what it is or they have an emotional block keeping them from pleasantly allowing themselves to be cared for. Receiving requires giving up control and gracious empty-handed acceptance.

The need to be in control

Perhaps there is some residual unworthiness contaminating my spirit, but here's the explanation I arrived at about reluctant receiving: In giving, I, the giver, am in control. But...when receiving, control is relinquished to the giver. Most of us like control. Some need it more than others. A few are addicted to it. Receivers are out of control when someone is giving to them.

My need to control, I think, contributes heavily to the unsettled feelings I get when being appreciated, honored or just plain offered a gift. I confess that I don't like the feeling of not being in control.

Receiving is harder than giving

Here is the event that woke me up and changed me into a more gracious receiver.

> Many years ago, when I was the solo pastor of a church in Iowa City, a young woman taught me a much-needed lesson about receiving. At the close of the Sunday morning service, I would greet the departing people. Some would offer words of appreciation for the service and the sermon.

My habit was to deflect all praise and compliments. I rejected as unneeded and unwanted any gifts that said, "That was excellent, meaningful and helpful." By body language or words, I politely scoffed at those who said I had done a good job of preaching that morning. I acted like I needed none of that.

Then one Sunday morning, when I once again rebuffed a "gift-giver", she turned sharply and looked me straight in the face. *"Why can't you just say 'Thank you',"* she scolded.

I was stunned. Immediately, I knew she was right and I was wrong. Weekly, I had taken her kind gift and trampled on it. Weekly, I secretly longed for encouraging words but showed no gratitude, acknowledged no neediness — just shoved away every gift offered, even though I craved each of them. My behavior disguised my hunger and denied her, and others, the pleasure of gift-giving.

I was permanently changed

From that Sunday on, I humbly responded, *"Thank you, I really appreciate that,"* whenever anyone offered positive words about the morning message. I'd been bulldozed into honesty, out of the un-genuine pretending I'd been practicing. I had been stopping those generous gift-givers by straight-arming their kind words.

When I was a Hospital Chaplain, I initiated a publication called The Chaplain's Newsletter. It was published quarterly and went out to clergy and board members of the hospital. One day I received a letter with just a few words clearly written on the one page. It read, "Your Newsletter is excellent!" It was signed by a man named Maurice TePaske, a board member from Sioux Center, Iowa. I was bowled over with the praise for my fledgling writing effort. I have never forgotten that gracious note and the man who wrote it. It encouraged me enormously.

I still sensitively take note of how gifts are received. I find myself bothered by Pastors to whom a compliment is paid for a job well done and they reply, *"It wasn't me, it was the Lord."* Because it sounds so humble, it is easy to miss the fact that it is another way of deflecting a kind gift and acting like it isn't needed or appreciated.

Let others say goodbye

Another version of misguided humility showed up recently. One of our valued long-time staff members decided to leave for a new opportunity. We regretted that she was leaving because we liked her personally and appreciated her productivity.

Suddenly she was gone. She scarcely said goodbye and rebuffed all ideas of a farewell luncheon. She just wanted to slip away.

That same way of leaving is sometimes seen in the plans of folks as they approach the end of their lives. They insist that there be no service for them when that time arrives. They just want to be cremated or buried, with no fanfare at all. The reasoning surrounding such ideas is often similar: they regard the attention paid them at a funeral or memorial service as unnecessary regard for a mere mortal. Having no attention paid to them is seen as proper piety— appropriately humble. "I am nothing. Pay me no heed. Just praise God."

The error in the thinking of the employee and the departing saint is that they are thinking of themselves, not those who long to say a proper, heartfelt goodbye. In both cases, selflessness would be to allow, endure and maybe even enjoy the attention for the sake of those left behind in sadness.

Several decades after my own learning experience, I'm still more comfortable giving than receiving. My natural inclination is for feelings that might be expressed with the words:

- Spare me from birthday celebrations where I'm the object of attention.
- Let me pass, when awards or honors are being awarded.
- I'll stay home when group photos are being shot.
- Even "thank you" notes make me nervous.

Nevertheless, these days I mentally override my initial inclination, and I actually do enjoy them.

Let others help

Consider this situation, where I was surprised to find myself both the giver and the receiver:

Before I could begin my seminar, I needed a portable podium moved to the front from the far corner of the room. Mindful of my gimpy back, I asked John Lotspeich to get it for me. He quickly moved it to the right place and sat down again next to me.

"Thank you, John," I said.

"No, I thank you," said John. *"Thank you for asking me to help you. I really appreciate being able to do something."*

I felt stymied about responding to the reverse spin John had put on my appreciation. I then saw that there is more to Care and Kindness than merely handing out assistance. Allowing others to serve oneself is another kind of graciousness. Allowing others to contribute meaningfully to me requires humility on my part and a willingness to turn over some control to someone else.

One of our Elders, Rowland Manson, shared with me that a woman in the church had asked him if he would stop by to visit a gravely ill relative.

Rowland responded by stopping nearly every day for a few minutes. Then Rowland added this: *"I am so honored that she invited me to do that. I feel so privileged,"* he beamed.

Care and Kindness is not just giving to others. We honor and affirm others when we ask for their help. When we enable someone else to give and reap the satisfactions always present in giving, we are handing them an unexpected gift. This is a way we can express our humility —by being willing to receive.

Empty-handed receiving

To truly enjoy "amazing grace" requires allowing honest neediness to creep into my soul. Earnest empty-handedness is being "poor in spirit". There lies a prime qualification for receiving spiritual help, as well as being equipped to gratefully accept the love and appreciation others want to give us.

We who major in giving care must be especially sensitive to this challenge — by giving a lot, we may lose our capacity to graciously receive, because we become so used to being in the driver's seat of giving. The secure position of giving becomes a comfort zone not easily given up.

The pain and constant receiving

A physically challenged woman in a wheel chair at our Care and Kindness Conference told me that decades of living with an irreversible condition has been an on-going lesson in how to be on the receiving end of care. *"It isn't easy,"* she said, *"being helped, needing assistance, not being independent."* Always being on the receiving end, she was implying, kills something vital to balanced living. She needed help, but constant need sapped her soul.

Caregivers need to hear this cry. We need to stay on-track, delivering what is needed, but carry high sensitivity to the ordeal of those who are on the receiving end much of the time. We can find ways of giving that preserve the spirit and dignity of the recipient.

The best way to fine-tune our "giving reflexes" may be to search our own souls—to assess how we feel when allowing gifts to come our way. Regular openness to the discomfort of letting another serve us or care for us — even asking others for assistance—may groom us spiritually in positive ways.

Jesus accepted gifts

Jesus' example, when he was anointed by an adoring woman with costly perfume, can help us. He graciously accepted what his disciples rebuked as wasteful. He took the gift and honored the giver. His spirit was lifted and she experienced the joy of giving. The most generous gift-giver of all was also a humble receiver.

Jesus treated people with respect. His words cut deeply at times, but still he left the confronted with personal dignity intact.

The human person is an intricate weaving of the physical with the spiritual. Dignity is a spiritual quality essential for a God glorifying spark. Strip away this essential fabric and the light of humanity is dimmed. Dignity includes a hearty sense of God-nurtured self-worth and a healthy self-respect.

When Jesus washed Peter's feet, the act challenged Peter's sense of the Lord's dignity. He thought such an action was beneath The Master's proper boundaries. Leaders, teachers, and mentors were supposed to remain aloof and above. Foot washing violated the traditional notion of superiority. Jesus turned a lot of thinking upside down.

A surprise ending to an act of care

In following what I thought was Jesus' example, however, I may have blundered seriously. Foot washing is tricky business, I learned. On the other hand, as Jesus showed, spiritual health includes the capacity to allow your "feet to be washed" by another. **cf. John 13:6–8**

I'd like to share a story with you in which I gave myself to another in an unusual way. I thought I was doing the humble deed. The result still baffles me. Here was an act of giving that I may have been wiser to withhold. See what you think. As you read, consider whether it was giving or receiving that caused this surprise ending. Or was this man's dignity bruised by my helpfulness?

"Scotty died Saturday." The news shocked me. I had just visited him on Wednesday. He hardly

appeared near death. Now that I think about it, however, I figure my visit contributed to his death.

Scotty was 85 years old when he breathed his last. I'd known him for nearly fifteen years. He was an active member of the Crystal Cathedral, where I serve as a staff pastor. It was always enjoyable meeting Scotty on the church campus, or anywhere else for that matter. His energy, enthusiasm, and natty attire radiated an infectious, upbeat, and encouraging attitude. Scotty lifted people's spirits. That seemed to be his mission in life in his retirement years. He loved to circulate around the Cathedral entrance on Sunday morning, and when other events were scheduled. He greeted, guided, and spoke words of cheer to guests and regulars. Scotty improved the environment conspicuously.

Scotty's manner disguised the pain in his private life: a chronically ill wife, serious financial difficulties, a costly swindle. Few knew. Few cracked through the pleasant exterior to the harsher realities. Most just enjoyed the outer man, one of life's cheerleaders, who preferred to lift others, preserve his privacy and keep up an appearance of well being.

I found Scotty

My final visit to Scotty was triggered by a growing consciousness that I hadn't seen him in a long while—five years, or more. Illness or death had not been reported, so I started searching. The phone number and home address we found in our records proved obsolete. The next alternative was asking folks who might know. Soon these efforts bore fruit. I traced Scotty to a nursing home not far from the church.

I found Scotty stretched out on his bed in a small, crowded, two-bed room. Fortunately, the other resident was out. Scotty recognized me and greeted me with a faint semblance of his characteristic pep. He raised himself from the bed, but while getting up, he interrupted his intention to settle into the wheelchair standing ready close by. *"I need to go to the bathroom,"* he said. And he commenced a shaky shuffle in that direction, with my support at his side. At the moment, this seemed a simple enough maneuver that I could lead him through, rather than summon an aide or nurse. *"Do you have to pee or BM?"* I inquired. *"BM,"* he replied, and turned, dropped his pants and underthings, and sat down. *"I'll wait in the next room, Scotty, take your time. Holler if you need help."*

After a ten-minute wait, I called out *"Do you need anything, Scotty?"* *"No,"* he replied. I waited another ten minutes, then walked over to see for myself. *"I'm finished, but I need some help,"* he said. Spotting a red Call Button, I pushed it to get the help Scotty needed to complete the process. Time passed. No one came.

A unique dilemma

By this time, nearly 30 minutes had passed since I arrived at Scotty's room. The length of this pastoral call, I could see, was stretching beyond my intentions. The pressure to move things along contributed to what happened next.

– 190 –

Another ten minutes passed with no help in sight. Finally I said to myself, "I should not be above wiping an old man. In the spirit of Jesus, who washed his friends' dirty feet, I should be willing to perform such a personal service." I got up, went into the bathroom, ripped off a generous wad of toilet tissue and took care of the need at hand, mildly proud of myself, though slightly revolted.

"Okay, Scotty, you can stand up," I announced. So he did, but to my dismay I saw at his feet a jumbled mess of undergarments and moist Depends. I went for help!

I returned soon with an aide at my side, who crisply and cheerfully put things back together neatly and promptly and delivered Scotty to the bedroom.

"Finally," I thought, *"we can talk."* Forty-five minutes of preliminaries had taken its toll on my plans for the day, but I decided to give prime attention to Scotty anyway. As we sat, I sensed Scotty avoiding looking at me. His head was slightly bowed, with his face turned away. His earlier fervor had disappeared. Now he seemed...well...the word came to me clearly five days later...depressed. At the time, I attributed the change to exhaustion from the bathroom ordeal. A brief, mostly one-sided conversation followed. I prayed, with his assent, and after assisting his return to bed, I departed, promising a follow-up call soon. But in three days, Scotty met his Maker.

Scotty died. Why?

When I heard of Scotty's death, so shortly after our experience together, I couldn't believe it. Stunned, I pondered what had happened that he would wind down so quickly. Gradually, I think I understood. I realized I might have played a part in his rather abrupt unraveling. Proud Scotty, I reasoned, had slipped down farther than his spirit could tolerate. The pastor had wiped his butt! How low can you go and maintain a sense of human dignity?

Scotty's boundaries had been violated. Had his meager, remaining self-worth been flushed down the toilet? He had endeavored to be a worthy churchman, standing next to the clergy, building the church. Now he sat reduced in his mind, I'm sure, to a helpless, pathetic patient.

My act was well intended, but perhaps wrong. Rather than being a help to him, it was an insult. When the pastor trespassed into his personal zone, it inappropriately drained away Scotty's fast-falling sense of personal pride. Rather than kindness, it proved demeaning.

When Scotty sat beside me with averted eyes, he may have been helped if I had offered an apology. Perhaps his spirit was already too badly bashed, but an apology was what I should have given.

Was his dignity smashed?

This drama revived in me the awareness of the spiritual nature of humankind. Much more than physical, a person lives on spiritual care, as well as bread and meat. Dignity is a spiritual commodity. Some depend on dignity more than others. All need some. Older people must be treated with high regard and elegant respect, with care that protects their sense of being worthy, valued human beings.

Advanced age, with its inevitable infirmities, too easily reduces folks to objects of care. Men and women with decades of service and accomplishment disappear into the crowd of dependent old people, little remembered for their lifetime of contributing. Such dehumanizing dehydrates the soul and kills the body as well.

Someone had to help Scotty with his bodily function need, but not his Pastor. Probably not even his own adult children, if avoidable. They, too, are key players in propping up his fragmented dignity. The best answer is the hired help. They serve as personal appendages to the infirm. Little loss or confusion of identity and dignity happens when elementary needs are serviced by aides and nursing assistants.

Tender care sees the person more than the wrinkles, the frailty, or neediness of our elders. Care for the spirit is a need more urgent than the temporary mistakes and messes that call for attention.

Scotty's pride may be faulted in this drama, too. Was Scotty, like Peter when Jesus crouched down to wash his feet, unable to accept a caring gift? Was his pride too brittle to let himself be cared for so personally by a Pastor?

Was it a blessing in disguise?

Another perspective on Scotty's sudden death is totally positive. Rebecca Caldwell, a ministering Elder at The Crystal Cathedral, sees Scotty as waiting for a final blessing; a caring touch from a Pastor. When that happened in the form of a visit, help with his bathroom needs, and a prayer, she believes Scotty was able to release his grip on life and move on into the presence of Jesus.

Giving and receiving are tightly wrapped up together. Generous giving requires gracious recipients. And every one of us is called to both. Those who want to help need those who allow themselves to be helped, and to graciously receive what is given. Plus, the very act of becoming a follower of Jesus depends on openhearted receiving, as well as giving.

The risks of giving

In the big picture of Care and Kindness, giving plays a prominent role. Those of us endeavoring to regularly and consistently give kindness away need to know there are risks involved. The generous gift is not always well received. We must also guard against indiscriminate benevolence that may violate. We are urged by Jesus to let our light shine in this world and humble giving is a leading way to do that. But, it must be thoughtful, sensitive and careful (as well as full of care). Humility is at the heart of both giving and receiving. The essence of humility is willingness to do what is needed.

Humility is a key concept

Why do we include a whole chapter on humility in a book on Kindness? Does it truly fit, in the sense of being a key component in this project?

The answer is "Yes, it is a foundational issue!" Along with "showing up", an understanding of humility has the potential to free people to greater production of loving kindness.

Stressing that "90% Of Helping Is Just Showing Up" paves the way for loving folks to reach out to the hurting. No excuses!

Correctly defining humility deprives any who would hide behind a pious shield, like claiming unworthiness or personal inadequacy. For example, "I'm too shy (or insignificant or young or old) to go up to (renowned musician, famous author, important theologian) and offer words of appreciation."

I was struggling to exercise humility with Scotty and to be totally willing to do even the most mundane task in my desire to show care, to show kindness, to meet his obvious need. Denying my personal comfortableness, I "died" for Scotty. Nevertheless, the humble act may have been wrong or misguided. What I did seemed to fit every criteria of a truly humble act. I discovered later that the personal dignity of Scotty was an overlooked variable.

Appropriate receiving may also be part of the Scotty story. Perhaps no one had ever scolded him to just say "thank you" when a kind act came his way. Maybe Scotty needed a little more "empty-handedness" in his spirit, so he could have received graciously the dignity-threatening act, rather than have it crush his spirit.

The words of St. Paul add encouraging thoughts to this entire issue. This is the classical reference called the "Emptying" passage. It is packed with guidance for each of us wanting to live as followers of Jesus.

If you have any encouragement
from being united with Christ,
if any comfort from his love,
if any fellowship with his Spirit,
if any tenderness and compassion,
then make my joy complete
by being like-minded,
having the same love,
being one in spirit and purpose.

Do nothing out of selfish ambition
or vain conceit,
but in humility consider others better
than yourselves.

Each of you should look not only
to your own interests,
but also to the interests of others.

Your attitude should be the same as
that of Christ Jesus:
Who, being in very nature God...
made himself nothing,
taking the very nature of a servant,
...he humbled himself
and became obedient to death...
Philippians 2:1–8

Obedience is responding to the cries, the loneliness, the neediness of those around us. That may define humility best.

Discussion questions for Chapter 8 are on pages 246–250.

ఇఇఇఇఇఇ

Kindness Example

Glen Gorman is a New Hope Telephone Counselor and a
training facilitator, as well. Glen also owns and operates an
auto body shop where bent and battered cars are brought
for repair.

Glen's staff, mostly men, who meet those who bring their
vehicles after a traffic accident, have been instructed to
listen to the stories about the accidents that caused the
damage.

Reflection: What a surprising idea this is, but so obviously
appropriate! Who needs to talk as much as one who has
just crashed his car or had it bashed? This is taking the
New Hope counseling training home and using it in
everyday life in a creative and useful way. I find what
Glen has his people doing very exciting.

ఇఇఇఇఇఇ

ৡৡৡৡৡৡৡ

Kindness Example

Dean Wilson says the Care and Kindness project has
inspired him to plant a kind attitude in his mind each day as
he sets off on his long trek to Koontz Hardware in West
Hollywood from his home in Huntington Beach. He
attempts to retain a caring outlook all the way and he finds
the trip flows smoothly and less stressfully when he
succeeds.

When he forgets and slips into anger and aggression as he
drives, he arrives irritated, upset and agitated.

Reflection: This is passive or invisible Care and Kindness.
It has to do with what doesn't happen, the stress that
doesn't show up, the frustration that stays away. For Dean,
it means controlling his attitude to keep his spirit peaceful.

ৡৡৡৡৡৡৡ

Kindness Example

This is a true Grandmother story from Pat Almeida:

Caitlyn, who lives in Pennsylvania, is 3 years old. She was adopted from China when one year old.

In her preschool, the teachers noticed Caitlyn inviting each of her classmates, one by one, to go somewhere with her. She seemed to be speaking of sleeping in a big bed, but told the kids they would have to take turns because they couldn't all sleep there at the same time.

At sharing time, Caitlyn was asked what her invitation was about. Caitlyn responded that she was inviting all the children to come to California to her grandmother's house. They asked her why she wanted them to come. Caitlyn replied, *"to get hugs and kisses from my grandma."*

Reflection: I've read research that claims children are naturally empathetic. This little Asian girl seems to prove those studies. No one taught her the desire to share the love she cherishes.

-9-

Moving Out Of Your Comfort Zone

It is easy for Care and Kindness to stretch us out of our comfort zone. Unfortunately, it is also easy to avoid. We must deliver Care and Kindness everywhere we go, and it almost always involves giving of some of ourselves or giving up something, even if it is only our sense of comfortableness or control. It requires effort that is easily bypassed or avoided. We must be willing to step into areas of discomfort or risky territory to deliver aid and encouragement to others. Most Care and Kindness requires putting one's self out a little—or perhaps even a lot. You might think of it in terms of "dying" for another.

You Too Can Die For Others

Dying for others can take many forms, but all ways require some kind of giving up of your comfortableness. In most cases, this is done in a direct or indirect effort to help another person. I believe this is the direction followers of Jesus must go.

The life of one of my best friends was saved recently by the courageous efforts of a small group of people. Some were his family members, but two key participants were his colleagues, acting exclusively out of love and concern. Not only was his life saved, so was his job, and probably his marriage. It was not a pretty event, the rescue operation, but it did work.

Those who managed this dramatic salvage may never be thanked or appreciated for what they did. They walked into the sanctuary of a person caught in the clutches of alcohol addiction and confronted him in every way imaginable. Cornered and pressured, his defenses crumbled and he finally agreed to admit himself to an alcohol treatment center.

They died for him

He, whose life was saved, however, is not pleased. In fact, he is angry, and the people who took part are now despised and rejected by him. They died for him and are paying a price for it (which can be part of the dying). They died for him by risking their friendship to confront him sharply in a way they hated. They died for him by overriding their terrible reluctance and fear and by challenging him face to face to get help. And they did it to save his job and his life.

There are few more dramatic examples than this. Ordinary folks acting out what Jesus wants, replicating in their own lives something of the dying for others that the Lord did for us in a major way. People have to do things like that.

If there is any theme running through the marching orders of Christian people, it is this: we are called to die for others. We are not to create insulated cells of safety or to live in our warm wombs of contentment. We are to find times, places, and ways of breaking out of the comfort zones in order to do what is needed.

> About twenty five years ago we were cruising through the state park at the Ogallala Reservoir in Nebraska in our family car, looking for a camping site. Idling along the dirt road, we encountered a

middle-aged couple running intently toward the water. I thought nothing, but my wife said they looked like something was seriously wrong. So I pulled alongside and asked if they needed help. Frantically, they pointed toward the reservoir. *"Our boy is under the water,"* they cried, without stopping. With that, I braked the car, jumped out, and took off running the same direction. Four kids and the dog were right on my heels, with Linda following.

You can't leave it to others

When I got to the edge of the water, a young boy was pointing and crying, *"He's in there; he's in there; he's in there."* I looked around the gathering crowd. The parents hadn't even arrived yet. I thought, "Somebody has to do something." But no else was moving. Instantaneously, it hit me. I had to do it. I stripped to my underwear in a flash and dived in. Nothing. I surface dived three or four more times. Nothing. Eventually, there was another man in the water, but, tiring dreadfully, I was beginning to fear for my own life. Seconds later, we made contact and together brought the youth to shore, where several volunteers now picked up the resuscitation efforts, though they proved to be futile, we learned the next day.

Circumstances forced me into action that day. I was compelled by the emergency to dive in; surprised that no one else was doing it! Seldom is life so clear. Usually we can assume, or imagine, some one else will do it.

Most of the time our inaction is not conspicuous or even noticed at all; doing nothing is lost in the crowd. It is easy and ordinary to stand back from that which requires risk, time, energy, and other forms of potential self-sacrifice. In the less dramatic events of life, where a neighbor is unemployed, an acquaintance has a death in the family, or a colleague's marriage breaks up, failure to assist or reach out is easily overlooked. Doing nothing is not always noticed, but…it is nevertheless a failure to reach out.

The funny thing is that dying for someone is life-giving for oneself. New, better life flows from actions that break us out of our insulated safety areas—if we survive. I nearly drowned at Ogallala Reservoir. That goes with all this. It isn't dying if there is no risk, no cost, no discomfort. Decades later, I still feel good about the Ogallala effort.

This is counter-culture thinking. That is, it is the opposite of everyday attitudes that advise us to bypass any challenge that incites feelings of discomfort. The conventional outlook is to avoid discomfort if it is not an obligation.

Life comes from death

Resurrection followed death literally for Jesus. That is unique. But there is an intrinsic life principal involved in what Jesus did. It is that the way to life always goes through death. This is a contrarian idea. It challenges radically our instincts to clutch security and grasp comfortableness rather than give it up and let it loose, at least now and then. Jesus calls us to lose our lives for his sake. The common value we are taught in the secular world is to save our lives, not lose them.

> A young woman consulted me about her dilemma. She was one of three adult children recently orphaned, so to speak. Her mother, the owner of a dress shop, had died, leaving the store to her, the

youngest daughter, but only small monetary bequests to her two siblings. She didn't feel it was fair. Part of her relished sole ownership, but her Christian convictions prodded her toward equity. Eventually she took legal steps to share everything. She died for them. She loosened her grasp on her inheritance and shared it with her sisters.

This kind of living through dying is not required of us. It is not the purchase price of a ticket to heaven. Heaven is a gift. New life always comes from some sort of dying. Dying for others grows soul. But more importantly, it is Kingdom Building; it is spreading God's Care and Kindness on the earth. It makes Planet Earth a better place because God is felt as more present.

That's why we're here—to make the world better, inch by inch, through personal acts of Care and Kindness, giving tastes of God.

The awesome power in letting go

Here is an example where two loving daughters had to give up what they wanted most, in order to love their mother appropriately. They had to die to their desires, hopes and wishes, in order to meet her at the right place.

Room 426 at the University Hospital looked like a cheerful, fun-filled, child's room in an affluent suburb. Colorful posters brightened the walls. Upbeat slogans on computer printout paper called for determination, hope, and willpower. Flowers in vases created a spring-like ambience. It was a picture of life, zest, and vitality. Two attractive young women rose to meet me at the door, both exuding radiant smiles and sparkling enthusiasm.

Outside the room, they asked if they could speak to me alone before I talked with their mother. Reluctant, but curious, I agreed. My well-trained early-warning system guessed what was coming. They wanted to head off any possibility that I might spread morbidity on their mother or in some way reduce or dilute her will to survive. They wanted her to live. They were determined she would live. I assured them that I would cooperate, so they released me to go to their mother's bedside.

Mother lay there like a patch of paleness in the midst of a field of color. Her weakness struck a dramatic contrast to the vitality of her dynamic daughters. She spoke softly. Her mind worked clearly. She immediately understood my mission and reached out a frail but warm hand of welcome. The watching daughters fortunately took me at my word and allowed me to visit alone with their dear mother. And mother proceeded to tell how the ordeal of illness wore on her. She felt so very tired from a long struggle with a failing heart. She wished now she could slip into sleep and wake up in the presence of Jesus. *"But,"* she said, *"the girls need me so badly. I guess I just have to hang on for them."*

Now it was my turn to call for a huddle. The lounge of the cardiac-care unit waiting room provided a good space. I wish someone else could do this for me, I thought, as we found our places to sit together. Exactly how we eased into my agenda, I don't recall, but we did. I gently suggested to the daughters that they consider letting their mother go. Predictably and understandably, I met resistance and Godly argument. *"It's wrong to just let her die!"* They are probably right, I thought, so I backed down a little, shaken out of my bold belief that their mother's whispered wishes ought to be honored. *"Well, think about it,"* I offered, as a parting resurgence of confidence welled up within me. I spoke a careful prayer. We parted.

In two days I returned. A different pair—the same daughters—met me. They appeared changed. The sisters greeted me with warmth but not with the high-level radiance of our first meeting. Again they asked for a consultation before I walked in to see their mother. She was sleeping anyway, so we stepped out into the hall.

Love turns

They had clearly heard what I said at our last meeting. They reacted with anger at first, they admitted, but as they talked together, they had begun gradually to realize it was their wish, their desire, that Mother should live. Not Mother's. Mother hung on to life for them. Enduring soul-searing weariness, she continued to cling to life for their sakes, because they begged her to. Tearfully, now, they acknowledged their entanglement in a powerful web of self-centered love that was blotting out sensitivity to their mother's needs. Prayer, they said, had changed their minds during the forty-eight hours since our original waiting room conference. Their enlightened love stood willing now to let Mother go. It was not what their hearts longed for, but they knew what was right. Fairness and love called for releasing her.

Now a formidable task awaited. Contrary to popular thinking, the capacity to stay alive or to give up life often rests in a person's own spirit, at least partly. Mother had decided to live, for the family. The young women understood their awesome assignment to go tell Mother they would be all right if she went to Jesus: that she could leave. Finished with my part, I excused myself. This was their personal, private, holy ground. They should walk it alone at their pace.

In the privacy of Room 426, Mother and daughters entered the most difficult task of their lives. It was agonizing, but they did it. Paradoxically, the mother brightened for a few hours after the conversation with her daughters. Then, only twelve hours later, peacefully slipped away to the brighter place waiting for her. And two loving daughters began to work through their grief. Heavy sadness swept over them, but modified and assuaged by the deep satisfaction of having walked through the valley of the shadow of death in the most meaningful way possible. Hand in hand they'd ushered the one they loved to a better place.

There is a time to fight

Letting go is not always the right answer. There is a time to fight, to hang on and rally all energy for another kind of win. Heaven and earth cheer such victories, too. Fighting for life or quietly moving on, can each be expressions of living faith.

Here, letting go was the loving answer. Ironically it involved <u>dying,</u> by the daughters, to their wants and wishes to let their Mother depart in peace. This is supernatural behavior, it is love that can only come from God, whether they knew it or not. It is the kind of giving up to which we are called.

Reluctant love delivers needed peace: Clarissa

My "Clarissa Lesson" was one I learned, in spite of myself. I reluctantly gave up my needed time of rest and recreation to meet the need of a woman who cried for help in a slightly offensive way. I gave up my time and limited energy for her in a superficial and deficient way—yet the results were surprising.

Clarissa had called the church, asking for a pastor to come visit her. The request was relayed to me about 9:00 p.m. on a Sunday. Dying was mentioned, so urgency surrounded the message. Tired, and weary from many urgent calls where I rushed out only to find the dying person watching television or reading the newspaper, I decided to telephone first.

Clarissa answered. She was okay, she told me, and, yes, it would be fine if I stopped by the next day.

Monday is usually my day off, but the hospital was a small one not far from my home, so I felt agreeable about a visit to Clarissa. Before departing, I checked with my office about the referral and discovered Clarissa, in her request for a pastor, had ordered that "no Blacks, Asians or women" should come. It was also noted that she was not a member of the church, nor did she attend.

Enthusiasm drained

Suddenly my enthusiasm for making this call drained. Instead, a chore loomed. I disliked this woman even before meeting her. The visit on my day off was shaping up as nothing more than a distasteful duty. I felt more than a little reluctant. I now saw her as a bigoted old woman who didn't even support the church, claimed she's dying, sounded strong, and was intruding on my precious free time and limited energy.

As I walked into her room, my distaste for her worsened. The distinct odor of cigarette smoke permeated the air. Here she is, I thought, supposedly on the verge of death from pneumonia, heart failure, and circulation problems, and she's smoking in her hospital room. And I'm supposed to be supportive, caring and interested. Everything she's being treated for is not only made worse by smoking, it probably caused it in the first place. Outward pleasantness covered my growing disgust.

Clarissa was sitting on the edge of her bed, looking even more alive than I'd expected. Just another non-urgent urgency, I groaned to myself. Although breathing with conspicuous difficulty, she asked if I cared if she smoked. *"I won't be staying long,"* I replied. *"Why don't you wait just a few minutes?"* She agreed.

I worked at care

Despite my prejudices, I worked hard at taking an interest in her. It turned out that she had been divorced at a very young age, left with two infant sons, whom she had raised as a single parent. One, now middle-aged, lived with her at the present time. The other, the youngest, had died a short time ago at age 53. She talked of her early life with obvious pain and sorrow. Clarissa had earned a living for herself and her children as a concessionaire at carnivals, fairs and other public events. She hawked baby turtles and chameleons, moving to a new spot weekly. I invited her to tell me all about it, and she did with some energy and manifest relish.

As I listened, I also heard within myself a distinct important voice: "You aren't able to enter her suffering. You blame her for causing her own ailments. You are keeping yourself at a distance. You have depersonalized her by being angry about her bigotry, addiction and unattractiveness."

The voice helped push aside the glaring defects that had been repulsing me. "She's a person, a hurting, suffering human being. This needy, frightened, dying old woman has had a tough life and is mourning her youngest son's recent death," my inner voice insisted.

A little progress

By the time our visit closed, I had managed to draw a little closer to her. My vision cleared, enabling me to see her as a child of God—yes conspicuously faulty, but reaching out as best she could for a word from God. Still mildly repulsed, I placed my hand on her arm, and offered a prayer. Her other hand promptly slipped over on top of mine in a clear show of appreciation for my interest and prayer:

"Thank you God for your presence with Clarissa in this very difficult time and for walking with her throughout her life. May she know you are with her now, that you love her, and that you will never leave her or forsake her in this life or the one to come. Bless her now with peace of mind. Clear away all fear and anxiety. Enable her to rest securely in your care, in Jesus' name. Amen."

After a silent moment, I stood to leave. She thanked me for coming, then directed me to put the chair back over in one corner and to bring up her bedside table. I complied, bade her farewell, and left.

The next day, I shared the aborted day-off story with pastoral colleagues, accenting my predominant irritation over the unenjoyable disruption in my day. I painted a picture of a demanding, unlikable, awful old woman. I kept to myself the inner drama that had helped me treat her, at least halfway, decently.

She died that night

Later that day, Clarissa's son called and talked with my secretary. His mother had died that morning. On her instructions, he had discharged her from the hospital and taken her home Monday evening, but then toward midnight she had asked to return to the hospital. She succumbed in the early hours of

Tuesday, about twelve hours after our time together.

Clarissa's son overflowed with gratitude for the pastoral call. He had never seen his mother in such a state of peace as that evening after he picked her up from the hospital. *"A calmness rested on her like the Spirit of God,"* he said.

The news hit me like a freight train. I was stunned. I felt sad, embarrassed, confused, relieved, surprised, chagrined, gratified.

<u>Sad</u> – she had died leaving a caring son but little else of a supportive community.

<u>Embarrassed</u> – for speaking about her in such a negative way, and so near to her time of death.

<u>Confused</u> – by the mixture of feelings and my mental inventory of whether I had rendered an adequate and appropriate pastoral ministry to her.

<u>Relieved</u> – for her sake that her suffering had been transposed to heavenly joy. Also <u>relieved</u> that I made the call when I did rather than postpone it, a tempting possibility I had dismissed, fortunately.

<u>Surprised</u> – both that Clarissa so promptly died after our conversation and that her son knew about the visit, appreciated it, and called us.

<u>Chagrined</u> – that I could be so critical of a sick old woman and jaded in my attitude.

<u>Gratified</u> – over the very positive response of Clarissa's son and gratified that in spite of my flawed outlook, I had been there for her in a deep and meaningful way.

I learned a lot

Later, I pondered the entire episode, wondering what I could salvage and learn from a striking pastoral event like this. Here's what I came up with:

1. The healing presence of God can be ushered in, with my help, even when I am stuck in a resentful state of mind.

2. Being present to people can have enormous spirit-affecting and soul-healing results.

3. Clarissa apparently experienced the personal presence of Christ, and the assurance of eternal security, just because someone showed up, listened, touched, and prayed.

4. There are many ways to avoid entering another's suffering, to stay at arm's length. One of the most common detaching methods works by seeing reasons for what is happening, and blaming victims for their predicament. We may distance ourselves by knowing how the suffering could have been prevented and being bothered that the person was indifferent about her health.

Clarissa's cigarette smoking did this for me. It was part of the justification my spirit used to stay at a distance from hers: *"I need not feel for her because she has brought it on herself through a lifetime of nicotine addiction,"* my unspoken reasoning said.

The second heart-hardening material I latched on to was the anti-minority statements made in her original request for a Caucasian, male pastor. *"Aha!"* said my heart, *"This woman is a bigot, deserving little love and only perfunctory care."*

A third barrier was her appearance. This dowdy, unkempt lady, with conspicuously smoke-dried skin, hardened by decades in the sun, looked unattractive. How much easier it is to care for beautiful people.

She taught me important lessons

Clarissa taught me some additional truths I had learned before, but which I fear I will never master. The primary lesson on this Monday was how the human personality regularly guards itself from entering another's world of suffering. One of the easiest ways to do so is to find fault with the other person. (Notice that God comes through anyway.)

Other lessons I found:

1. Clarissa found peace without a push or sell, just by being treated with respect and by having poured upon her the promises of God.

2. She may have been waiting for last rites, or a blessing, in order to let go of this life.

3. God came to Clarissa and gave her His peace, even though she was bigoted, self-destructive, and not a churchgoer.

That adds up to quite a few lessons from one brief encounter. My best teachers have always been God's people—bent, bashed and broken. My rendezvous with Clarissa will always be a reminder of how a little <u>dying</u> on our part can pay major dividends.

It is a natural instinct for us to constantly strive to move out of our discomfort and into areas where we are much more comfortable. But there are so many acts of kindness that should be undertaken. We must resist the easy path of avoiding them with some excuse or another. We must be willing, at the very least, to show up and to allow ourselves to be a vehicle for God to bless others.

It's not about you

This incident, related by Marilyn Duff, illustrates how her daughter, Ann, discovered for herself that, 90% of helping **is indeed** just showing up. Not only did she show up, but she managed to keep the focus off herself as she made herself available for each of those who needed someone to lean on.

Ann R., a young mother of two, had seldom been exposed to others' grief. She'd avoided funerals and wakes with excuses of not wanting to intrude or not knowing what to say. But when, early one morning, she heard that the mother of her best friend had died after a lengthy battle with cancer, she knew something was expected of her. So she picked up the phone and called the house.

Her friend answered the phone and said that she and her three sisters and father were alone. Her voice was full of tears as she related how her mother had died peacefully—hadn't seemed to suffer. *"We're waiting for the funeral home to come and get Mother."*

Ann was filled with pain and sorrow as she listened—not only for the death of a mother who had laughed and joked with teenage girls and whose life was now over, but also for the family she had grown up knowing: the strong father who was now so devastated, and for this friend who was usually the first one to diffuse a situation with a joke. There was no laughter in her voice now.

"What can I do?" said Ann.

"Just come over. Please. Come over."

So she went, dreading what she would see. Dreading the tears and pain. Dreading the sight of a father in grief. Dreading seeing the mother, still on her deathbed. Afraid of her own reactions. As she pulled into the driveway, her heart was pounding, but she told herself, *"This isn't about you."*

At the door, the stricken family embraced her, and, as she held her and cried, she felt her friend's shaking body. Tears filled her own eyes, too. She wiped them away with her hands as they led her into the bedroom, and Ann saw that the mother looked peaceful and free of pain—for the first time in a long while.

Then they went into the living room and settled onto the sofa. What was she supposed to say now? But then she heard her own words again, *"This is not about me."*

The family talked of the long night and the relief they felt for their mother. Ann listened, not sure of what to say, so she just murmured or shook her head. The doorbell rang. An uncle arrived, looking nervous and ill at ease. The dad introduced him, then took him away to see the mother.

"Oh, thank you for coming," said her friend, squeezing her hand. The three sisters thanked her, as well. Their gratitude for her presence surprised her. She had expected to be in the way, but nothing seemed to be further from the truth. They seemed genuinely glad to have her there.

She sat with them as they talked. The father returned with Uncle Bob, who looked ashen. The uncle tried to change the subject to traffic on the freeway, but his voice was a little too loud, and his hoarse laughter was met only with polite and subdued smiles from the sisters. Every now and then, one of them would sob and bury her face in a tissue.

The doorbell rang again; the hearse had arrived. As the family rose to go to the door, Ann sensed that it would be the hardest time for the family. She also sensed that her own presence in that room at that moment was not necessary, so she got up and went to the kitchen.

She leaned on the sink and took a deep breath. *"Why am I here?"* she wondered. *"What am I supposed to do now? Should I stay? Should I go?"*

Suddenly she noticed that the sink was full of dirty dishes. There were over-flowing wastebaskets, pans on the stove with the remnants of past meals. Almost without thinking, she ran hot sudsy water, and began scraping and loading dishes into the dishwasher. The noise of running water almost blocked the sound of painful wails and wrenching sobs in the background. The body was being removed from the bed, transferred onto a litter and carried to the waiting hearse. Ann plunged her hands into the sudsy water.

She checked the clock; it was past noon. She went to the refrigerator, removed lettuce, lunchmeat, and bread; arranged platters and baskets; put water on the stove for tea; filled the coffee maker;

and got out ice and glasses. She unwrapped a plate of chocolate chip cookies, with a card from a neighbor attached, and set it on the table, too.

Then someone entered the kitchen. It was Uncle Bob, who plopped down at the kitchen table, and began to talk nervously about how rainy it had been lately. She asked him what he did for a living and where he lived. Uncle Bob opened up, and his voice lost its strain. They chatted as Ann set the food on a table, found paper plates and stacks of napkins.

In a little while, the family returned to the house. When they saw the impromptu buffet awaiting them, they exclaimed their gratitude, and as they went through the motions of filling their plates, they calmed, seeming to breathe a bit easier, to forget their pain for the moment in the simple routine of eating.

"Maybe this is why I am here," Ann thought, following along in the lunch line. *"To hold people and let them cry, to be a listener for people who need to talk, to put a little order to chaos.*

In any grieving household, there would always be people like Uncle Bob, who simply needed some place to escape to. It had not been so difficult after all. In fact, her heart had never felt so full. *"Maybe it was a little about me, too,"* she realized.

Most excuses cover the fact that we do not want to become uncomfortable; we avoid that which we are too anxious about and uncertain of. Ann was a worthy Ambassador of Kindness as she did what was needed, even though she was uncomfortable and uncertain.

As we respond to the call to deliver Care and Kindness, let us dare to move out of our comfort zones. When we do, we will carry the love of God into needed places. Hungry people will be nourished by the taste of God that our humble efforts bring.

Discussion questions for Chapter 9 are on pages 250–252.

Epilogue

If you have read this book, your life must be changed for the better. The vision of showering kindness around you each day is about making a greater difference in this world. Everyone can do more and everyone must. Staying the same is not acceptable.

If you are a teenager or younger; if you are a young adult or an older person; if you are in retirement or living in Assisted Living, you are drafted into the Army of Jesus to become a consistent encourager, a constant voice of thanksgiving, a steady song of appreciation to those around you. You have new marching orders to connect with the weary, call on the ill, reach out to the stranger. You are called to "show up."

No matter what your age, you now have a fresh vision of your reason for living—it can never be taken from you. This purpose in life guarantees that you will always be needed, wherever you work, play, rest or study. Until your dying day, you can actively express to anyone around you words of Care and Kindness that will strengthen their Hope.

PRAYER: "Lord, show me today how to help another person. Lord, cancel my shyness and any reluctance that stands in the way of giving someone today a taste of your goodness. Help me, Lord, to be humble, so I worry less about how I look and more about giving to others. Lord, write on my heart a new motto of Care and Kindness to guide my life. AMEN"

After the prayer, read the following Scripture to bolster your confidence and strengthen your resolution. Make these words your own:

The Spirit of the Sovereign Lord is on me,
because the Lord has anointed me
to preach good news to the poor.
He has sent me to bind up the broken hearted,
to proclaim freedom for the captives
and release from darkness for the prisoners,
to proclaim the year of the Lord's favor...
to comfort all who mourn, and provide for those who grieve...
to bestow on them a crown of beauty instead of ashes,
the oil of gladness instead of mourning
and a garment of praise instead of a spirit of despair.
Isaiah 61:1–3

Discussion Guide

-1-

They Will Know We are Christians by Our Love

1. There are enormous possibilities every last follower of Jesus can participate in and help with—simple down-to-earth acts of care and kindness.

    A. List as many down-to-earth acts you can think of that would demonstrate Care and Kindness.

    B. How do acts such as these improve the lives of people around you?

2. Being a follower of Jesus is not just about having a ticket to heaven. It is not just about feeling forgiven, saved, redeemed or thankful. It is not simply about feeling anything, even though powerful feelings often nourish one's spiritual life.

    A. Why is being a follower of Jesus not about having a ticket to heaven?

    B. Why are feelings not the only part of being a follower of Jesus?

    C. Do you think it is important to feel forgiven, saved, redeemed or thankful? Explain.

3. Suffer with him? To suffer with Christ means—at the very least—to be going about our everyday business intentionally taking risks to deliver concrete acts and words of Care and Kindness.

    A. Do you feel you are suffering with Christ?

    B. Does your everyday business involve suffering? Describe it.

    C. How can it be risky to deliver acts and words of Care and Kindness?

4. He reaches out to other men and takes them on sailing trips, meets for breakfast with a small group of peers and enjoys a new marriage. His story is so powerful for all of us. To realize that our routine conversations, asking about another's family or work, playful jousting and jesting, friendship and compassion, in the context of Christian living makes a difference.

    A. How do our regular activities and conversations make a difference to others?

    B. What can make it difficult to inquire about another person's life in the context of Christian living?

    C. How is it possible to jest and be playful and still be a positive influence to others?

5. My God-given mission is to fan the flames of love in the hearts of Jesus followers and hopefully start a prairie fire of conspicuous deeds, actions and behaviors that will make the world a better place. I want to inspire and convince good people to do a little more, consistently, and intentionally. I want them to go into difficult places where the hurting, the

sick, the bereaved are. More than that, I want them to be sprinkling kindness everywhere they go on those who do not necessarily look needy and discouraged.

    A. Try to articulate your own mission.

    B. How would you feel about going into difficult places to visit the sick or bereaved?

    C. Why do people who don't seem to be hurting or discouraged have the same need as others to be shown Care and Kindness?

Putting it into practice

Start today a project for the rest of your life.

When you are in a room where someone teaches, performs vocally or with a musical instrument, presents a dramatic act, prays, shares or amuses, make a direct personal contact afterwards.

Thank the performer and affirm him or her for what was presented.

-2-

Five Key Essentials to Encourage and Motivate

1. Essential Key # 1   I have the capacities, qualities and abilities that can brighten another's life, or help them face challenges.

    A. What capacities, qualities, and abilities do you recognize in yourself?

B. How do you actively express these abilities?

C. Do you think that everyone truly has these capacities, or are some people just not made that way?

2. <u>Essential Key # 2</u>: Everyone needs my encouragement and support. People need to be noticed personally and respectfully by me and given some word, gesture, or look of appreciation.

A. Does everyone need encouragement, or are some people sufficiently self-confident?

B. What are some ways that you can notice people in a personal, yet respectful, manner?

C. What words and gestures are in your vocabulary to encourage others?

3. <u>Essential Key #3</u>: Care and Kindness, whether it is my smile, a word of thanks, a visit, or treating another fairly, builds hope and happiness in that person's heart and opens them to God's love.

A. How can an act of Care and Kindness build hope for someone?

B. Isn't God's love a Christian concept? How effective are acts of kindness toward non-Christians?

C. Suggest a hypothetical situation where you encounter a grumpy, pessimistic person. Describe what you would do to express Care and Kindness.

4. <u>Essential Key #4</u>: Care and Kindness toward anyone is Care and Kindness to the Lord.

A. Why is Care and Kindness toward an atheist, who doesn't believe in the Lord, not a waste of time?

B. In what ways does this Essential Key stimulate new ideas for you?

5. <u>Essential Key #5</u>: Care and Kindness is infectious. Others catch it and Pass It On.

A. Describe a situation where you found that an action you took was contagious.

B. Do you think of being part of a chain in "passing it on", or do you view acts of kindness as one-at-a-time things with specific persons?

C. How does someone's act of kindness toward you affect your actions toward others?

Putting it into practice

Give a compliment to everyone who helps or serves you in the course of today's activities. Like this:

"You have a nice smile."

"I like your name."

"You are such a good worker."

"You are a sharp dresser."

If you prefer to hint that you are a Follower of Jesus, make a practice of wearing a Cross or Angel pin on your clothing.

-3-

Where Is God In All This?

1. Caring folks do truly (some of the time) so closely identify with others that their hearts ache for them and with them. The capacity for this differs from one person to another.

    A. How much capacity do you feel you have to truly feel another's pain and hurt?

    B. How can a person who feels limited in this capacity still be caring towards those who need support?

2. Compassion is a central quality in the essence of human beings.

    A. If this statement is true, how is it that some people don't seem to show this quality?

    B. Do you feel that compassion is a natural expression for you, or do you feel that you have to work consciously at it?

3. If you claim or name no feelings, you are not one who has the ability to empathize.

    A. How do you reconcile this statement with the traditional image of the "strong, silent type"?

    B. What instances can you recall where you have denied yourself the expression of feelings?

    C. In your own family, are feelings generally expressed openly or are they suppressed?

4. If I find myself face to face with the brokenhearted, but my feelings fail to engage, am I a suitable care-giver? When appropriate words come out of my mouth but internally I am dead or detached, should my care-credentials be revoked? Must I feel another's fear, sadness, discouragement, in order to "show up" and effectively speak or pray with them?

    A. How do you answer the questions raised in the paragraph above?

    B. Do you feel that you are like most other people or that you are different in you ability to engage your feelings?

    C. If feeling another person's hurts is not a litmus test for caring, then how can you effectively speak or pray with them?

5. When I as a Pastor am at the bedside of someone going through an agonizing ordeal, I feel little. My brain is working over time as I see the difficult struggle.

    A. What would you say to people who worry about their mind being too active when they feel they should be listening more passively?

    B. Do you think being analytical and keenly observant is an aid or impediment to being effectively supportive?

    C. Given the choice of submerging yourself in compassion and empathy or remaining cooler emotionally, which do you think is better? Which are you more likely to do?

6. To survive very long as a warm caring person, some distancing is necessary. With little or no capacity to stay somewhat at arm's length, as was mentioned earlier, the courage to continue will soon diminish.

    A. Why isn't "staying at arm's length" contradictory to being a caring person?

    B. How can you distance yourself and still be effective in expressing love, care and support?

7. Truthfully, it is impossible to feel another's pain precisely. We can be touched by her distress; or his tears can trigger ours. But when we do feel very strongly in the presence of someone else's heartache, it sometimes means the situation is stirring up old distress of our own.

    A. What experience comes to mind where you were really dealing with your own history and pain, rather than the distress of the person you were trying to help?

    B. What should you do when old, painful memories come to the surface during your caring efforts? Suppress them or permit them?

    C. How do you deal with the realization that you are rehearsing your own hurts but others are interpreting your emotions as being empathetic to someone else?

8. The author related the story of the two small children, Cody and Courtney, and drew a comparison with the Biblical tale of Hagar and Ishmael.

    A. What elements of these two situations are similar?

    B. How are these two stories dissimilar?

C. How did God reveal himself in both cases?

Putting it into practice

When illness or adversity enters the life of someone you know or with whom you are slightly acquainted, make a call on the telephone and say:

"I heard about your special challenge and I'm concerned for you."

After you let the person talk, saying only a little yourself, add, *"This must be difficult. I'll be praying for you."*

Conclude the call after the other person responds.

-4-

Just Show Up

1. The more common thought, when the challenge "to care" is brought up, is concern for those who are seriously ill, in deep grief, or going through an unusual difficulty.

   A. Describe the different views of offering care that you have after reading this chapter.

   B. What is your concept of "caring"? Does it involve serious issues and tragedies?

   C. How do you describe what it means "to care"?

2. In 1996 the book entitled **90% of Helping Is Just Showing Up** arrived on the scene. The title became the theme of a Care and Kindness Conference, now held annually at The Crystal Cathedral. The reason that the "showing up" idea was latched on to was its relevance for promoting lives and behaviors of care and kindness.

    A. How would you describe "showing up" in practical terms?

    B. How have you made a conscious effort in the past week to "show up" for someone else?

    C. Why is showing up so important?

3. We claim that caring is for amateurs. Definitely there is a place for professional caregivers. We need counselors, therapists, social workers and pastors who sit with the distressed and help them move ahead when tough times set in. But Jesus depends mostly on amateurs to show loving kindness in this world.

    A. Do you consider yourself an amateur?

    B. Describe situations where an amateur can be more effective than a professional.

    C. Why does Jesus choose to rely on amateurs?

4. "Showing Up" takes many forms. Some are so simple… People are thankful for acts of kindness, no matter how little.

    A. Name different ways you can show up.

    B. Is showing up always simple?

    C. Why does it take courage to show up?

5. It was an upbeat article that was prominently placed in the periodical and I was paid for the piece and expected nothing more. From the thousands of readers, however, I received the surprising gift of two letters thanking me for what I had written. Two showed up! I had not expected any.

    A. Why was the writing of a letter a way of showing up?

    B. Why do you suppose that so few people take the time to send a note of appreciation?

    C. How are these forms of appreciation a gift?

6. There is a time to break the "just show up" law. There is a time when Care and Kindness takes the opposite turn. There is a time to not show up.

    A. In what kinds of situations would it be best to not show up?

    B. How can it be considered caring to not show up?

    C. What guidelines would you set for yourself in deciding whether to show up or to not show up?

Putting it into practice

When you learn of a death in the family of anyone you know, even a slight acquaintance, call on the telephone:

    a) Identify yourself clearly.

    b) Say, *"I have heard that your brother (mother, cousin, dad, grandfather) died. That is so sad."*

c) Let them talk.

d) Finally say, *"I wanted you to know you are in our thoughts and prayers, and we know a death like this is very sad."*

-5-

It's Sunday, but Monday is Coming

1. Sunday is a day of rest and refocusing. Then on Monday morning Jesus' people should be ready to go out with renewed energy and ideas.

    A. What has been your view of how we should think of Sunday?

    B. What connection have your Sundays had with the six weekdays that follow? Explain.

    C. How much responsibility should a member of the congregation take toward being renewed and refreshed vs. it being the responsibility of the minister and other worship leaders?

2. On our vacation this summer I heard two excellent sermons in two different churches.

    A. What kinds of sermons do you typically hear?

    B. What kinds of sermons would you like to hear?

    C. How do you think your effectiveness at spreading Care and Kindness during the week can be affected by the Sunday sermon?

3. The toll-taker had dispensed a taste of God to Donna. Thoughtful words like his are part of the species we call love. Love comes from God. I had a similar experience exiting the Budget Car Rental lot in Chicago one winter day.

    A. What experiences have you had where strangers have done an unexpected kindness?

    B. How do you think the gesture made by the toll-taker was received by other drivers?

    C. What do you think other people would think of you if you used the words "have a blessed day"?

4. I consistently make eye contact, smile, use their names when a name tag is present, and in parting, hand over a compliment or words of appreciation. It is easy to do.

    A. What would stop you from trying experiments such as this?

    B. Do you greet strangers in public, or do you keep quietly to yourself?

    C. Do you agree that these small efforts are easy to do, or are they hard for you?

5. A commitment I have made is to consistently approach speakers, performers, musicians, teachers and others, when possible, after they have made their presentations.

    A. When have you expressed your appreciation to someone following a presentation or performance before a large crowd?

    B. Do you think public performers receive enough compliments and adulation?

C. Why would you feel hesitation or shyness about approaching such people?

D. How are these forms of appreciation a gift to the performer? What percentage of performers do you think appreciate such gestures?

6. It is simple but it does require constant thoughtfulness. It easily slips away in the hurry and busy-ness of everyday living. But I am committed to it and find that it is becoming habitual and almost automatic the more I do what I should.

A. To what extent are you willing to make a commitment to do daily, thoughtful acts?

B. How can you remind yourself to keep the commitment and guard against getting too caught up in your everyday routine?

C. Do you think it can ever become habitual, or does it always require conscious effort?

7. During the whole time, you are in fact totally preoccupied with this gray behemoth, but in the interest of courtesy, you say nothing.

A. Name times when you have avoided talking about the elephant in the room.

B. Why do you think people tend to not speak about the elephant?

C. Describe a time when you leaned around the elephant, but in hindsight you can now see that it would have been more helpful to have brought it up.

8. On United Airlines Flight 125 from Chicago I had the great fortune of garnering an exit row seat which for my 78 inch frame is heavenly. Across from the wide exit area was a jump seat where the Flight Attendant would sit as we took off or landed.

    A. Discuss this entire incident. Do you think it was intrusive to inquire of the Flight Attendant?

    B. Do you think the Attendant was receptive to having someone show care and concern?

    C. Do you think it was mere "good fortune" that there was so much time available for the Attendant to be able to talk?

9. I was the hurting party with fresh bereavement. He was a veteran of long past losses. I had cracked the door of lament open, but he walked in, paying no attention to my concerns.

    A. Have you ever been guilty of being much more interested in relating your own story than listening?

    B. Why do you think people fall into this trap repeatedly?

    C. In what way is telling a story of your own helpful to someone who has suffered a crisis?

10. When we pray or promise prayer, we remind people of that connection and we use it for their well-being. We personally go to God and ask for help for the hurting person.

    A. What hesitations do you have about praying in front of another person? Have you offered to include a prayer in your visits?

B. Have you ever caught yourself casually telling someone you will pray for them, or saying, *"I'll pray for you."* as an automatic comment, rather than a sincere intention?

C. What evidence have you personally seen of the effectiveness of praying with someone for their personal need?

Putting it into practice

Calculate how you can show kindness during the six days of the work week.

Think of a half dozen people to whom you can speak, make a phone call, or send a note of interest, concern or appreciation.

Make the call or write the note—one each day.

-6-

Allow, Accept, Affirm, and Appreciate My Feelings

1. At the very foundation of the concept of caring, there lies a principle that feels counter-intuitive. At least counter to most of our past experiences. That principle is this: allow people to feel their pain. Don't deny them this necessary step in healing.

A. In what ways does it bother you to let people fully feel their pain?

B. How do you think that pain is part of healing?

C. When should we do what we can to stop another's pain?

2. It is plausible that our earnest attempts to help another feel better are really based on our own discomfort with upset feelings. In other words, if I can get you to act and talk more cheerfully, I will feel more comfortable and less upset.

    A. How uncomfortable are you in the presence of someone who is distressed?

    B. What do you think about attempts to cheer people up to help them forget their troubles?

    C. What "pat answers" can you think of that are commonly used to diminish another's grief?

3. Many people act as if they believe that they can create an atmosphere of healing by renaming the "bad stuff".

    A. List some examples where you have renamed a negative problem.

    B. What examples of that do you see in our society in general?

    C. Forest Lawn Cemetery and Mortuary calls the end of life ceremonies "Celebrations of Life" instead of funerals. What are your thoughts about this way of speaking of these sad events?

4. Why should we allow the person to feel the pain of his problem? Why not put a "spin" on it so the blunt pain of the blow is softened?

A. Do you typically try to look on the bright side of each situation? Why do you do that?

B. How do you separate being positive minded and being caring enough to allow people to feel their pain?

C. When are you able to "let the tears flow"?

5. My old friend, if I interpret his behavior accurately, totally miscalculated my condition. I was loving the memories he was sharing. I valued the tender feelings evoked. I loved the tears welling up in my eyes. No apology was needed.

A. In what encounters have you felt badly or guilty when your "comforting words" have caused another to cry?

B. Did you apologize at those times? How did the other person respond to your apology?

C. When another "tears up" in your presence, how do you react?

6. The "don't cry" exhortation ought to be blotted out, erased, eliminated.

A. When do you tell family or friends to not cry?

B. How did you feel when someone urged you to not cry?

C. What does "weep with those who weep" mean to you now?

7. Other ways to weep: Get inside the other's feelings as much as possible. Show that you feel or understand her

distress. To put it another way, do not move quickly to try to fix another's problem. Hold back your remedies.

    A. What are the ways you can weep with a hurting person?

    B. Describe how suggesting a solution to someone's problem is not actually helpful.

    C. Why do you think we are so quick to offer remedies to a person in distress?

8. I like to teach people to listen with their "third ear".

    A. What is the third ear?

    B. What are clues that the third ear can pick up?

    C. What responses can you give when you notice something with your third ear?

9. The trouble is that few will tell us directly what they are feeling. They talk about what happened, but seldom add how they are feeling about it.

    A. How do you help someone who does not speak as if they are in distress when in fact they are?

    B. What is the hazard in getting caught up in the facts surrounding a crisis?

    C. Is there ever a time when you can ask the questions that are burning in your mind about a particular crisis (like, "was he wearing a helmet")? Should you avoid those questions and not speak about the particulars of the event?

10. Tragedy triggers sympathy and compassion for hurting ones, but another's triumph brings forth jealousy—a primal

human fault so readily aroused. Truly dancing for joy when success pours down on a peer, but not on us, calls for a supernatural effort to override our envy.

    A. Discuss whether it is easier for you to 'weep with', or to 'rejoice with'.

    B. If it is hard for you to sincerely enter into someone's great joy, why do you think that is?

    C. If your neighbor, or your sister-in-law, or your co-worker won the lottery, would you truly be glad for that person?

    D. Describe a situation when you failed to "rejoice with" and how you think you could handle it better now.

11. Those who move into joyous achievements claim that it is rare for people to see and share their joy at a level that resonates positively.

    A. How can you share someone's joy without sounding insincere?

    B. Do you find people suspicious when you show too much enthusiasm about their successes?

    C. To what extent can you exaggerate when sharing someone's joy?

12. *I have a problem. I want to tell you about it. No, I really don't. I'd rather keep it to myself; handle it alone.*

    A. How can you reassure someone that you want to walk alongside him with his problem?

    B. How can you encourage another to open up and share with you when he is feeling afraid of being vulnerable?

C. How do you rate your willingness to listen and love, without trying to "fix"?

Putting it into practice

Greet people heartily with a smile everywhere you go—in your neighborhood, in the halls of your workplace or school, at the shopping mall, and everywhere else you find yourself.

-7-

A Daily Diet of Care and Kindness

1. One day, Linda, my wife, said, *"We ought to have a checklist we carry or post on the refrigerator for the special acts of Care and Kindness we deliver every day."* We need teach ourselves to take inventory daily on how well we have done that day, was her point.

    A. How could having a checklist such as this help you?

    B. Do you keep track of other things daily, such as nutrition choices, counting calories, exercise, taking your pills or flossing? Explain.

    C. As you think back over the past week, how many items could you put on your Care and Kindness checklist? Name them.

2. There are two important things about Care and Kindness. The first is that a life-style that shows compassion and concern for others helps the one delivering such goods. Secondly, and logically connected, is that those who receive Care and Kindness are healthier when their spirits are lifted by kindness and encouragement.

    A. Why does showing compassion and concern affect your own health?

    B. How do you think the recipient of an act of Care and Kindness is affected?

    C. Can you think of things other than health that may be affected by showing compassion and concern?

3. As most children raised in Christian homes are encouraged daily to say their prayers, and clean their plates, we want them schooled in doing good works every day.

    A. How realistic is it to think that children can be taught to do good works every day?

    B. Why would some think that being caring and being kind is kid's stuff?

    C. How would putting a checklist on the refrigerator help achieve this goal?

4. Let's bring up our children to regard no day as complete without checking off the special efforts of Care and Kindness extended. To do this well calls for adults to model such living.

    A. How can adults model Care and Kindness living?

    B. Do you think children would respond only to the modeling of their parents, or can other adults also be instructors in the teaching of Care and Kindness?

C. Don't you think that today's children are too caught up in themselves to effectively learn to think of others? Discuss.

5. Belief needs to be expressed. It must be demonstrated! "Faith without works is dead," again quoting James. That means that being a child of God requires showing loving kindness to the world. It calls for behaving in uniquely gracious ways all the time.

A. How can we demonstrate our beliefs?

B. Do you think it is possible or wise for us to be gracious <u>all</u> the time?

C. How can our vocations and avocations be an expression of our beliefs?

6. Here is what one of our country's most famous psychiatrists, Karl Menninger, said when fielding a question from an audience after a lecture on mental health. The question was, *"What would you advise a person to do if that person felt a nervous breakdown coming on?"* Most expected him to say, *"Consult a psychiatrist."* To their astonishment, he replied, *"Lock up your house, go across the railroad tracks, find someone in need and do something to help that person."*

A. What do you think of this psychiatrist's advice?

B. If you feel a nervous breakdown coming on, shouldn't your own health take priority over worrying about other people?

C. Why would finding a person in need be helpful to your own mental health?

7. As every minute of the EKG had a time printed on it, they then went back and tried to see what was going on with the patient at that moment of his hospital situation. Their painstaking efforts yielded surprising results. They discovered that most often, … the patient was being cared for by nursing staff in some hands-on kind of way.

    A. Does this report surprise you? Why?

    B. Why do you think touch and attention affected the EKG recording?

    C. Have you thought about how much you can affect other people through a touch, a hug, a smile, or a kind word?

Putting it into practice

Post a blank sheet of paper on your refrigerator. Write <u>Today's Acts of Kindness</u> at the top of it. At the end of the day, list the acts of kindness you intentionally delivered from morning until night.

Repeat the exercise every day except Sunday.

-8-

Generous Giving May be a Sign of Humility

1. The word "humble" conjures up mental images, most of which are not attractive. We see timid, shy folks, with self-deprecating mannerisms that say, "Don't look at me, I am nothing."

A. How do you define or describe being humble?

B. How do you reconcile being humble and yet willing to step forward to fill a need?

C. Are you a person who can see what needs to be done, or do you wait to be asked?

2. The truly humble are not excessively preoccupied with self and having to look good or appear humble. They are characterized by seeing what is needed and stepping forward to try to meet the need.

A. What needs are around you that you could do something about, if only you had the courage?

B. When someone assumes a voluntary position of leadership, do you admire her, or do you think she is too assertive?

C. How important is it to you what others think of you and how they perceive your actions?

3. A humble person can ask "dumb questions". He doesn't have to already know everything.

A. Do you speak up and ask questions, or do you keep quiet so as not to look dumb?

B. When you run into someone whose name you should know, but you can't recall it, what do you say?

C. When Jesus spoke of seeing the mote in your neighbor's eye but not the beam in your own, how does this relate to humility?

4. When it comes to Care and Kindness, those who spread such goodness are the humble. Everyone carries a reservoir of positive thoughts, reactions and qualities.

    A. Describe what is in your reservoir.

    B. How do you keep your reservoir replenished and filled?

5. Learning to graciously accept a gift is another evidence of spiritual maturity.

    A. How do you feel when given a compliment? How do you react to the gift giver?

    B. When you compliment someone on something they've done, do you feel better if they act humble and embarrassed, or if they show that they are enjoying the remarks?

    C. How does accepting the gift of a compliment have anything to do with spiritual maturity?

6. I find myself bothered by Pastors to whom a compliment is paid for a job well done and they reply, *"It wasn't me, it was the Lord."*

    A. Relate incidents when you have heard a pious response to a compliment.

    B. Do you think that people who respond piously are being sincere, or do you think that they believe that is the proper response that they should give?

    C. What would a better response be?

    D. When paying a compliment, do you realize that you are giving a gift? That it could be just the gift someone needs? Discuss the dynamics involved in offering a compliment.

7. The same way of leaving is sometimes seen in the plans of folks as they approach the end of their lives. They insist that there be no service for them when that time arrives. They just want to be cremated or buried, with no fanfare at all.

    A. Is this the way your elder family members have stated their wishes? Describe.

    B. What are your feelings about the type of treatment you want at your own death?

    C. Do these feelings come from a concern about yourself or a concern about those whom you will have left?

8. In giving, I, the giver, am in control. But…when receiving, control is relinquished to the giver. Most of us like control.

    A. Is control an important issue to you? Describe.

    B. Why do you think abandoning control has something to do with humility?

    C. How hard is it for you to admit to neediness?

9. The author related a story about his time with Scotty in the nursing home.

    A. What thoughts went through your mind as you read this story?

    B. What would you have done if you had been the one visiting Scotty?

    C. Do you feel that this encounter was a disaster and a wrong judgment, or do you feel, as Rebecca Caldwell opined, that Scotty was waiting for a final blessing and a caring touch from a Pastor?

D. Discuss Scottie's part in allowing this unusual encounter to dispirit him.

Putting it into practice

Say to everyone you do business with on the telephone:

"Thank you for your helpfulness."

Or, *"I enjoyed working on this with you."*

Or, *"You have a pleasant voice."*

Moving Out Of Your Comfort Zone

1. Dying for others can take many forms, but all require some kind of giving up of your comfortableness.

A. Does your own desire to remain in a comfortable or safe place prevent you from responding to those who need you? Describe the impact of your own comfort zone on reaching out to others.

B. If you are the hurting person, how do you feel about asking others to step out of their comfort zones to help you?

2. The conventional outlook is to avoid discomfort if it is not an obligation.

A. Are caring acts an obligation?

B. Describe how being a caring person is counter to the culture of looking out for yourself.

C. How is moving out of our comfort zone equated with Kingdom Building?

4. The author shared a story from Room 426 at University Hospital.

A. Have you ever been a part of dilemma like what the two daughters were facing? Describe it.

B. Do you feel that the words of the daughters to their mother at the end of the story hastened the mother's death?

C. How do you think the daughters now view the lesson they learned, looking back at it with hindsight?

3. The author also related a tale about Clarissa, who called from the hospital that she was dying.

A. What feelings did you have about Clarissa as you read the story?

B. What conclusions would you have made after learning of her sudden death?

C. Do you think this is a unique story, or does it represent many occasions where we are called upon to help the "unlovely"? Explain.

4. Ann was a worthy Ambassador of Kindness as she did what was needed, even though she was uncomfortable and uncertain.

A. Even if you have not been a situation exactly what Ann faced, describe a time when you felt that you should do something, but you didn't know what to do.

B. Do you think what Ann did was truly exceptional, or could you have done the same thing in her place? Describe the feelings you would have had.

C. What lessons have you learned from this book that could have helped Uncle Bob?

Putting it into practice

Write a note of appreciation to:

Your dentist

Your physician

Your plumber

Your Pastor

Your employer

Your newspaper delivery person

Your mail deliverer

Your church organist, choir director or music leader.

Your veterinarian

Your security personnel

More Kindness Examples

When giving his order at the Taco Bell drive-in speaker, Mark told the person taking the order that he would pay for the three cars in front of him.

Reflection: This was a fresh and higher risk act modeled on the well-known legends of those paying fees for those behind them on toll roads and bridges.

Mark was giving a virtual blank check to Taco Bell, as he had no way of knowing what the bill would add up to. But the excitement of this anonymous act of generous kindness made it worth the risk.

Even though the idea was not original, the impulse toward kindness in Mark was genuine and generous. He wanted to impact strangers with a spirit-lifting gift in the middle of a busy day. He'd caught the spirit of what life is supposed to be like for followers of Jesus. He was acting "outside the box" of his daily work and busy schedule. Mark was not just concentrating on a noon meal; he was thinking of people and how to bring a smile to their faces.

After the Sunday service at her church Mandy made a special effort to locate the minister, a visiting pastor, who had preached the sermon.

When she located the pastor, she waited and then approached with her words of appreciation for the message.

The guest pastor simply said *"Hello"*, heard the words Mandy brought, and then promptly turned away.

Mandy had brought kind words—but she felt rebuffed, brushed off, slighted.

Reflection: This experience illustrates that acting kindly is not guaranteed to be noticeably appreciated. Some people cannot accept compliments or do not know how to receive a gift with poise. Others are rushed or get pulled away and the gift-giver feels snubbed, as Mandy did.

So intentional Care and Kindness must push on past the hurts and embarrassments that one's efforts sometimes elicit. Giving loving-kindness is good for the world, even when an individual may not accept it properly.

It is almost a law that you cannot tell how much your Care and Kindness is appreciated by the way the recipient acts.

Barbara Barrientos thought up a creative approach to Christmas this year. She and Ray have three adult daughters who usually shower them with gifts. Barbara asked the young women to bring no presents at Christmas for once. Instead, she requested they find a way to do something for someone in the form of helpfulness, rather than material things.

Their gift to their parents would be telling about what they did to brighten and assist others.

Reflection: What a joy it can be to creatively think up new ways of letting our light shine in this world. Things are small and fleeting compared to actions, the memory of which last a long time.

Larry Ball shared how his parents would drop him of at the Methodist Church on Sunday mornings. They then went off shopping.

Already, at ten years old, Larry liked being in church. The sermon fascinated him and the choir in the loft captivated him as well.

In the choir, one woman especially drew his attention. She was always there and he noticed her week after week for the years he attended. Then one day she was not there. He missed her badly. It wasn't the same. Church was incomplete. Then he learned she had died and he was deeply shaken. He grieved her for many months.

Larry had never met her; yet they still had a relationship. She didn't know it, but she played an important role in his emerging life of Faith. She was his encouraging friend, even though they never spoke to each other.

Reflection: What a powerful thought. That we might be an influence on someone we never even talk with or meet. This choir member's kindness was literally in "just showing up" and looking attractive.

Glenn De Master lives in a nice neighborhood where a few of those around him lack fluency in the English language.

One morning, as Glenn stood by his car, a woman walked by, so intent that she didn't seem to notice him. He said,

"Good morning", but there was no noticeable response. Another day as he backed out of the driveway, she looked at him as she was walking by. He greeted her, but there was still no reaction. He attributed it to her apparent newness in this country and a lack of English skills.

A few days later, she was standing on the corner where he turns, so Glenn opened the window and waved, but there was no response. The next morning, as he approached, he noticed his "friend" sitting there on the curb, so he waved to her once more, and then noticed from his rearview mirror that she got up and walked away after he had waved and turned.

From that day on, he would often see her sitting there on the curb, as if waiting for him to come by and bless her with a wave. After the wave, he would see her get up and continue walking.

Reflection: There is no kind action so minor that it can be discounted. The loneliness in this world is so common and widespread that the mere wave of a hand could be the warmest gift in another's day.

The long wait in the Dermatologist's office stretched longer and longer. The patients, bound together in a common ordeal, began to voice their irritation. Finally a young mother, baby in her arms, began to leave.

"I'll come back another day," she said, "the baby needs nursing soon."

Then a gracious soul, about to get her turn with the doctor, offered to trade places with the young woman.

The gloom of the whole group turned to smiles.

Pastor Ken Leestma brought back a remarkable story of Care and Kindness from the time he and Bette served in Bahrain as missionaries at the Reformed Church mission.

A physician, by the name of Paul Harrison, was caring for the indigenous people when a Bedouin chief brought his seriously and mysteriously ill son in for treatment. Dr Harrison diagnosed the problem; there was a circulation shortage in the lad's brain. *"What is needed,"* he said *"is a vascular transplant."*

This meant taking a healthy blood vessel from another person and transplanting it in the deficient brain of the youth. The doctor asked the Bedouin chief and his wife if either would donate a vein. Both firmly declined. So Dr. Harrison operated on his own arm and took his vein for the procedure.

Before the surgery to implant the vein, the Bedouin Chief warned the physician that if his son dies he, the doctor would die, too. An armed guard standing nearby emphasized the seriousness of this threat.

The surgery was a success. The youth recovered and Dr. Harrison's self-giving act became a legendary testimony of the love of Jesus Christ in his followers.

Reflection: This is high level selflessness, a kind of dying for another, in cutting himself to save the youth's life. Real Christ-likeness.

Ruth Gross was hurrying to her Sunday morning class when she ran into Ken. He mentioned that he had just buried his partner of many years, three days earlier. Ruth immediately dropped her plan to attend class. Instead, she went with Ken and sat with him during the early church service.

Reflection: So often, our agendas control us. If I am supposed to be a certain place at a specific time, that is where I am going to be. To drop my agenda and meet the need in front of me is an act of unusual grace and mercy. Too often the schedule controls us, rather than we the schedule.

Ruth's altered plan parallels the parable of The Good Samaritan. There, two men were due at the Temple of God. That seemed far more important than crossing over to aid a wounded man and risk disappointing people waiting for them at the place of meeting.

Meetings are often controlled by time and a task to get done. Now and then a sensitive chairperson takes a few minutes to check with the people assembled to discern how it is with them today. Such canny leadership exhibits a Kind and Caring concern that is not ruled by the agenda. Actually, more will get accomplished in less time when people are cared for first.

Marilyn Duff had a hard time finding a certain shade of lipstick. After finding one at Long's Drugs, she tried several other Long's stores. Then, finally, one woman gave her the number of the distributor of the lipstick line. Marilyn called the distributor, but didn't get any response for weeks. When the man finally responded, he said he had found several for her, and he sent all he had found, no charge. Two weeks later, another package came with seven more and a note "I got lucky this time".

Reflection: What a lesson in goodwill. Marilyn, and we who read this too, will never think anything but good about Long's Drugs. They passed by a little revenue but reaped tons of positive regard in turn. Whoever made those decisions sent a message that there is generosity and goodness in this world. That is hope-raising behavior.

Larry Bacon and his wife, Charlotte, own a flower business. At the end of the day, they usually have flowers left over. One day, they noticed a sign announcing a "family reunion", so they stopped and took a bunch of sunflowers to the door, saying they were for the family reunion. They said they were from a friend of the family.

Reflection: The Bacons are making the world more beautiful every day by selling flowers. This is what we are in this life for—to make the world a better, more hospitable and lovely place. Obviously making money is not the whole story for two people who would stop and give flowers to strangers having a party. These are good people!

Dr. Mark Spee was in an airport shuttle on Sunday night. He noticed that a woman tipped the driver and then another one did the same. One man didn't even have any luggage, but he tipped the friendly driver anyway. When Mark got off, he said he wanted to tip, too. It was infectious.

Reflection: Drop a good deed and the ripples go out and out indefinitely. Start an infection of kindness and others catch it and spread it everywhere they go.

Barbara Hokinson was in Office Max, arranging to have some office furniture delivered. When the salesman wrote down her address, he noted that it was the scene of a recent horrific accident. She told him that she had witnessed the accident. He stopped what he was doing, took her hands and offered a prayer for her, the families of the victims, and the young men.

Reflection: In the world of Care and Kindness, this salesman took a high level risk when he reached out in prayer to a stranger. But his aim was not misguided. He found a willing and understanding recipient. Care and Kindness is often risky. There are no guarantees. But followers of Jesus are willing to take the necessary risks, even though sometimes a door may be slammed in their faces.

While in Las Vegas, Margil Wadley was approached by a young man (maybe age 30) who spoke no English, but was neatly dressed and groomed. Margil could only understand his saying, *"I very hungry"*, so he motioned for him to follow. He took the young man to a sandwich shop and told the server to feed him, gave the server $9.00, and then left.

Reflection: Margil had no way of knowing if the man had already been fed four times that day. He took him at his word and did what he could, rather than hesitate for fear he was being hoodwinked. Care and Kindness is cautious, but not always meticulously on guard to prevent someone from taking advantage of them. Care and Kindness takes the opportunity at face value here.

When Edith Burkes got home from the hospital after a bout with pneumonia, a dear Christian brother and sister called her husband and told him to set a table for four. Rowland and Yvette Manson showed up with potato soup and bakery bread, further enhancing her recovery.

Reflection: Loving care and hot soup is the best medicine available.

Stephanie Soto, age five, said, *"My friend fell and hurt her head, I said, 'I hope you are okay.'"*

Reflection: Stephanie "showed up" for her young friend and spoke appropriate words of concern. She is on her way to a life of loving kindness.

Joanna Bushendorf's mother has been in a nursing home for the last 3 years, due to 3 strokes. When the weather is nice, Joanna looks forward to getting her mother outside. Most of the residents never get to go outside, unless a visitor takes them, so when Joanna takes her mother out, she goes back in and brings out as many others as she can.

Reflection: Sad to say, not all mothers have caring daughters. Joanna saw the others as if she belonged to them. This is a unique expression of "loving your neighbor as yourself."

Boyd Cowen made a bunch of decals that say, "and all God's people said ...WOW ...www.crystalcathedral.org" and gave them to Pastor Leesma to give to the church, either to sell or to hand out.

Reflection: This is "thinking outside the box", by a businessman who creates and sells banners and other promotional products. Now we know how this striking decal originated.

Frances Smith says, "*I always have home-made chicken noodle soup in my freezer to bring to someone I hear is sick.*"

Reflection: Could there be anything more appreciated than hot soup when you are feeling miserable? Here is a warm and wonderful premeditated expression of compassion and kindness.

Joe and Vera McInerney's grandson, Jonathan, takes the trash barrels to the curb every week for each of his neighbors. After school he puts them back where they belong. The trash man is his buddy.

Reflection: This ordinary kindness is extraordinary when a school boy is the one doing it. His kind deeds certainly reflect a family where helpfulness is a strong value. Thoughtful youth usually affiliate with thoughtful parents and grandparents.

About eight years ago while attending church, Jack Hadley's wife, Lou, started a conversation with a gentleman sitting next to her. She learned that he was a recently divorced clergyman visiting from Scotland. He was extremely depressed, almost suicidal, and uncertain what to do with his life. Lou invited the man home to dinner with them, where she discovered his blood pressure was extremely high, since she was a nurse. He was taken to Emergency, where an M.D. prescribed medication for the high blood pressure.

The visiting Pastor returned to Scotland, but the Hadleys remained in contact through e-mail, U.S. Mail, and a subsequent return visit. He is happily remarried, restored in the ministry, and he and his lovely wife have visited from time to time. He even attended the Institute for Successful Church Leadership at the Crystal Cathedral. He says Lou Hadley saved his physical and spiritual life.

Reflection: Lou's actions were simple hospitality and sincere concern. Anyone can do that, but Lou actually did. The Pastor's life was saved because she noticed his stressed look, spoke to him and cared about him. She offered him the Miracle of Kindness.